Antony Young is President of Optimedia International in the United States, a media agency that specializes in integrated marketing communication strategies. Antony has had a truly international career with ZenithOptimedia Group that includes launching the China company, heading the Asia regional operations and being CEO of its UK group before taking up his current position. He has worked globally on brands including Sony, Coca-Cola, McDonald's, HSBC, Procter & Gamble, Toyota and Nokia. He also co-founded a digital marketing company.

Lucy Aitken is a freelance writer specializing in media and marketing. She was previously editor of *Campaign* and *Media & Marketing Europe*.

PROFITABLE MARKETING COMMUNICATIONS

A GUIDE TO MARKETING RETURN ON INVESTMENT

ANTONY YOUNG & LUCY AITKEN

KOGAN
PAGE

London and Philadelphia

To Nancy and Dorian

Publisher's note
Every possible effort has been made to ensure that the information contained in this book is accurate at the time of going to press, and the publishers and authors cannot accept responsibility for any errors or omissions, however caused. No responsibility for loss or damage occasioned to any person acting, or refraining from action, as a result of the material in this publication can be accepted by the editor, the publisher or any of the authors.

First published in Great Britain and the United States in 2007 by Kogan Page Limited

120 Pentonville Road
London N1 9JN
United Kingdom
www.kogan-page.co.uk

525 South 4th Street, #241
Philadelphia PA 19147
USA

© Antony Young, 2007

The right of Antony Young to be identified as the author of this work has been asserted by him in accordance with the Copyright, Designs and Patents Act 1988.

ISBN-10 0 7494 4942 X
ISBN-13 978 0 7494 4942 1

British Library Cataloguing-in-Publication Data

A CIP record for this book is available from the British Library.

Library of Congress Cataloging-in-Publication Data
Young, Antony.
    Profitable marketing communications : a guide to marketing return on investment / Antony Young and Lucy Aitken.
        p. cm.
    Includes bibliographical references and index.
    ISBN-13:   978-0-7494-4942-1
    ISBN-10:   0-7494-4942-X
  1. Marketing--Management. 2. Capital investments--Evaluation. 3. Rate of return.
4. Profit. I. Aitken, Lucy. II. Title.
    HF5415.13.Y69 2007
    658.8--dc22   2006039729

Typeset by Saxon Graphics Ltd, Derby
Printed and bound in Great Britain by MPG Books Ltd, Bodmin, Cornwall

Contents

Foreword

Creativity and innovation should be at the very heart of any marketing and communications organization worth its salt. They certainly have always been at the core of what we do at Publicis Groupe. If we are doing our jobs right, we must never forget that the work we do... needs to work. And by working, of course, we mean that our creative ideas must deliver a payback – with interest – on the investment our clients make. Our clients demand – quite rightly – that their marketing efforts not only deliver results, but a real and quantifiable return on investments. This ever-higher degree of accountability, this focus on ROI, is changing the face of our entire industry.

That is why this valuable study which treats marketing communications as an investment is so timely. It adds to the momentum of a debate about marketing and about marketing's role as a key facilitator of business. Any executive from the CEO down who cares deeply about the success of his or her company should be taking part in this debate. This book demystifies marketing communications and explains how it can bring tangible financial results to the bottom line.

There are few people in the industry better equipped than Antony Young to explain the importance of ROI in marketing communications. I first came across Antony back in 2001, while he was running ZenithOptimedia in Hong Kong. He seemed to have a real knack for running media communication agencies because he instinctively understood that the essential role of the ad business is about getting results for clients. I was happy to see that a lot of clients apparently agreed with him – and Zenith was able to add assignments for P&G, Coca-Cola, McDonald's, Sony and others under Antony's stewardship in Asia. Antony helped establish Zenith's value proposition as 'the ROI Agency' – and this later became the mantra for the entire international network. Delivering business results through marketing communication was a need marketers all around the world were clearly demanding. He later applied these principles to UK clients with considerable success and has now taken his brand of management style to Optimedia US.

Books about ROI and marketing tend to be academic and full to the brim with the kind of jargon that makes this vital subject matter difficult to access. By going to the crux of the matter – how marketing communications can be profitable – Antony and his co-author Lucy Aitken make this topic incredibly accessible to readers from any background in the business world.

By examining marketing communications strategies with the approach of an investor, the authors have come up with a simple but powerful perspective. The investment and marketing worlds are furthermore interacting more than ever. Investors and analysts are increasingly interested in understanding how effective marketing can add shareholder value, while marketers and the agencies they work with are beginning to understand the implications of being able to demonstrate a quantifiable return.

When I agreed to write the foreword to this book, it was not to please the authors. It was because I have seen with my own eyes how ROI has worked for our clients. In the fragmented media world that is before us, with all the difficulties of reaching the right audience at the right time, we need to have a rigorous approach to media. The lesson of this book is that there is no single recipe. There are tools, some very specific, and proprietary, some less special, which when well used can deliver great results.

And you know what? We have seen this happening day after day. And our clients have been able to measure it, particularly when they shifted their business from another shop – wherever it was. The ROI delivered has always been superior.

Creative minds associated with skilled and rigorous spirits can create something new, fresh and unparalleled. This book is one such creation.

Maurice Lévy
Chairman and CEO, Publicis Groupe

Preface

As I sit in my living room watching the news, I sense it's going to be a rough week on the investment front. The newsreader reports that the S&P 500 is down 51 points in today's trading. My financial adviser tells me this isn't a great time to be seeing clients. 'We're at the mercy of the market', he says, reaching for a brochure for a Latin American growth fund. 'This should be a better bet in the long term.' I tell him I don't need to be told to invest in more or better funds; I need to know whether to invest at all, and if there are investment vehicles other than funds that will get me a better return.

Replace the word 'investment' with 'marketing'. Those funds are ads and media schedules, while those working in the ad industry are the investment advisers.

Marketers are generally good at recommending strategies to spend their budget wisely. Yet the big question for companies is: 'Should I be marketing at all?' Their boards' focus is on growing earnings, so they seek more meaningful results beyond ad awareness, cost per acquisition or branding.

Marketing is still seen by many companies as a cost rather than an investment. It tops the list of types of expenditure most likely to go in a downturn.

There are two key reasons that explain this predicament. Firstly, company boards have lost confidence in marketing. Upgrading new stores, improving distribution logistics, trade incentives and price promotions are seen as better alternatives to traditional marketing. Secondly, many marketers have failed to demonstrate a clear line of sight between marketing and the bottom line.

Companies need to improve their management of marketing communication portfolios. They need to understand better the potential return of different channels – ie direct, event, PR, digital, promotions, trade marketing – in reaching out to customers and the level of risk associated with strategies. If marketers are able to demonstrate ROI from marketing, then CFOs won't cut budgets.

This is the thinking behind *Profitable Marketing Communications: A guide to marketing return on investment*. This book offers a unique perspective to marketing by introducing investment disciplines and strategies to marketing practices. It offers insight into how marketers have delivered outstanding Marketing ROI for their companies. Finally, it provides a blueprint to maximize returns from marketing communications.

This book will be an invaluable source for marketers to help drive growth and profitability. In addition, it's a reference book for non-marketing executives to improve their knowledge about how to work with marketing in terms of evaluating, challenging and engaging it to deliver improved business performance.

Acknowledgements

One of the early inspirations behind 'The ROI Agency', which was to become the mantra adopted by ZenithOptimedia, germinated from a chance breakfast with Austin Lally, the then general manager for Procter & Gamble Greater China at a hotel in Guangzhou early in 2002. He recalled thinking as a young brand manager that marketing was all about making TV ads, and in contrast comparing this to his current job that involved shutting down local factories to enable the company to reduce the price of Tide to compete effectively against the Chinese laundry detergent brands. In his native Glaswegian accent, he then went on to lament how agencies were preoccupied with developing the creative work and recommending media plans, but struggled to understand clients' business issues.

That provided a fascinating insight into the real challenges facing marketers. Marketing ROI became a mission that we would pursue in subsequent years at our agency. I met some remarkable marketers and agency people who showed thought leadership in this area and provided invaluable material for *Profitable Marketing Communications*.

I'd like to thank Frank Harrison, Derek Morris and Andrew Green at ZenithOptimedia and Ingrid Murray of Ninah Consulting, who without doubt are among the cleverest people I have worked with and whose interest and views on the subject matter enriched our understanding of it. Also Bruce Goerlich, who gave invaluable input from the other side of the pond. I 'd also like to thank Steve King for bringing me to London, supporting this book project and then deciding to move me to New York, thereby accelerating the writing of this book; and Gerry Boyle for giving me his backing to building our ROI agenda for the UK agency. I'd also like to single out Katrina Lodge for her dedicated support over the entire project. Thanks to the many at ZenithOptimedia and Publicis Groupe who contributed to the research.

My admiration goes to the many clients that practise true marketing ROI. Specifically, I'd like to acknowledge Julian Elliot, Bernhard Glock, Giovanni Fabrice, Susie Moore, Russ Shaw, Paul Philpott, Andrew Singer, John Sills, Ian Edwards, Woody Hardford and Rob Rees who lent their time and access.

We'd like to acknowledge the IPA, the WARC and the advertising and media agencies that supplied a large body of material through the published IPA Effectiveness Awards, which we were able to reference for this book.

I must thank Helen Kogan, our publisher, who from day one saw the potential ROI for this book and gave excellent advice and encouragement to see it through.

I can't thank enough Lucy Aitken, my co-author and partner on this project. It was a real delight to work with her. This book simply would not have made it without her. Her ideas, energy and talent gave this book enormous authority and colour.

Finally, thanks to my wonderful wife Nancy, who soldiered on through last summer, managing the house, making travel arrangements, packing, overseeing renovations, dealing with realtors and arranging kids activities single-handedly as I selfishly hid myself upstairs all those weekends in our loft in Wimbledon, 'finishing off that bl... book!'

1

A need for a new marketing model

In June 2006, United Airlines announced a restructure that included a $60 million cut in marketing and advertising. At the time of the announcement, Robert Mann, the president of R.W. Mann & Company, an airline industry analysis firm in Port Washington, New York, told *Brandweek* that the airline intended to rely on newer media that would be 'far more efficient'.

Mann's comment sums up a groundswell of support for alternatives to mass marketing that are thought to deliver a better return on investment. Why would a company spend millions on mass marketing when it cannot ably demonstrate that the return on investment is worth it? Surely it would make better business sense to spend that money on other investments that justify the outlay?

Increasingly, United Airlines is the rule, not the exception. In 2005, the world's biggest advertiser, Procter & Gamble, cut its TV budget by 8 per cent. Considering that P&G's global marketing budget is £6 billion, this had huge ramifications for the world's TV networks on which ads for P&G products from Flash to Fairy appear. In the same year, on a smaller but nonetheless significant scale, Heineken beer shifted its £6.5 million UK advertising budget out of TV and into sports sponsorship.

Marketing has become the runt of the litter in the modern boardroom. It's evolved into an expensive extra, the sunroof not the chassis. In many cases, it's not perceived as making a valuable contribution to the bottom line. It can't hold a candle to an impressive operations manager, a sales team under strong leadership, or a non-executive director who can offer impartial advice.

Marketing's reputation has taken such a beating that many companies now ask themselves whether they should be bothering with marketing at all, as opposed to vacillating over how much they should be spending.

Within many organizations, this culture has come about because marketing is regarded as a cost, not an investment. And, quite simply, costs are there to be cut.

More accountable investments are usurping marketing. For consumer goods, improving distribution logistics, trade incentives and price promotions are regarded as far more worthy of resources than marketing. Coca-Cola, for instance, may be the world's most valuable brand – with a value of $67 billion according to Interbrand – but a huge contributing factor in its success has been a franchise business model that sees local partners handling production, bottling and distribution.

It's easy for a board of directors to see the advantages of a clever distribution strategy, a profit-share scheme or a store revamp. But it's much less clear to see how a company will derive value from marketing. One reason why is because many marketers fail to demonstrate a clear line of sight between marketing and the bottom line. The marketing department increasingly risks looking like an anachronism in a business environment where ever more emphasis is placed on accountability.

This book argues the case for a new marketing model, one that helps business owners, CEOs, CFOs and marketers to apply an investment-led approach where the focus is value, not cost. Changing the mindset towards marketing by showing how it can generate value will, in turn, drive corporate growth and profitability.

A second function of this book is as a reference guide for non-marketing executives to help them improve their understanding of marketing and how it can drive growth within an organization.

HOW IT USED TO BE...

Many years ago, when it was still a young industry, advertising was considered to be something of a glamorous art. As the number of consumer products began to swell in post-war capitalist societies so did the amount of advertising. Adspend was directly proportional to consumer confidence: when consumers spent more, companies followed suit.

From the 1950s, television sets became more commonplace in the home, and mass-market advertising found its natural habitat. In the corporate world, as transport and infrastructures improved, consumerism grew at a furious rate. Advertising aided and abetted this growth.

The 1970s, 80s and 90s saw a golden era of marketing. Budgets were big and ad agencies churned out TV ads and bought space on networks through their in-house media departments. At the other end of the chain, aspirational consumers bought the products in ads that successfully seduced them. The United States sold images of the domestic goddess saving the day with Scotkins Paper Napkins or All Detergent Suds, appealing to women as homemakers. In the UK, Katie did the same for OXO.

When colour TV was present in most homes, the wasp-waists and the perfect hairdos of the 1950s and 1960s were eclipsed by a more down-to-earth image of family life. The everyday trials and tribulations of the OXO family were a fixture on UK TV screens for 16 years throughout the 1980s and 1990s, repeatedly selling an image of desirable domesticity through a meal enhanced by the stock cubes.

Victor Kiam, who liked Remington shavers so much that he 'bought the company', became a household name, while Nick Kamen sinking into a bathtub clad only in a pair of Levi's 501s lent the required sex appeal to a brand of jeans that temporarily devastated the competition. And, according to John von Radowitz in his article entitled 'Coffee romance reaches the boil' published by PA News on 7 December 1992, sales of Nescafé's Gold Blend in the UK increased by 40 per cent between 1987 and 1992. This boom in premium instant coffee was largely thanks to the soap-opera style 'will they, won't they?' dynamic between the couple in the ads, dramatic tension matched only by Ross and Rachel in *Friends* a few years later.

Marketing campaigns such as Gold Blend, Levi's and Remington worked efficiently because mass media meant mass audiences. When a campaign became newsworthy enough, it stretched its tentacles into the press and, eventually, into public consciousness. The ultimate accolade was when a slogan entered the vernacular. Beer brands have been particularly adept at this: 'refreshes the parts other beers cannot reach', 'reassuringly expensive' and 'king of beers' all accompany brands that have been carefully built over a long period of time. Nike's Just Do It and, more recently, McDonald's I'm Lovin' It are global examples.

I Love Lucy, Dallas, Dynasty and *Happy Days* were shows that worked their magic in the United States, captivating audiences in their millions. Companies bought advertising space from TV networks to build mass awareness for their products and services. Audience measurement techniques were employed to estimate ratings – still the currency for planning media campaigns to this day.

TV built brands and sold products, so marketers based their TV spend on 'share of voice', aligning a brand's advertising budget with its market share. The biggest headache faced by advertisers was how to keep up with rapid and regular rises in media inflation. TV companies all over the world, in recognizing their own strengths in reaching consumers, capitalized on their power to reach consumers in their millions.

The success of a particular ad was measured on the basis of day-after recall, a tool that became more sophisticated as ads' ability to communicate and persuade was honed. Reach and frequency became standard metrics.

As TV's might grew, attention to other media dwindled. Generally speaking, a brand wasn't a brand unless it was on TV; only a handful would risk not taking this tried and trusted route. TV spots were the cornerstone of most campaigns; appearances in other media tended to be add-ons.

Giant consumer packaged goods advertisers such as Procter & Gamble, Coca-Cola, Unilever and Nestlé became lead marketers. They recognized the power of television and reinforced the message that marketing worked, that it was a worthwhile investment. They showed how TV could jump-start a brand into life, give it momentum and sustain its appeal.

Marketers never had to justify their budgets or develop metrics that made sense to the finance or accounting people in their organization. It was a given that marketing worked; 'accountability' just wasn't part of the corporate lexicon.

Part of the evidence for proving that marketing 'worked' came from more consistent consumer behaviour. Research companies could track and measure attitudinal changes towards brands, giving companies insight into how tastes and trends were evolving.

On account of advertising enjoying such a meteoric rise, there was negligible debate about how to define – and much less about how to measure – returns on marketing investments. That legacy has been hard to shake. Indeed, an entire advertising and media industry – a global business worth \$403,663 million in 2005 and destined to grow steadily to be worth \$478,943 million in 2008, according to estimates from ZenithOptimedia – was built to support this infrastructure.

Today, the language of marketing assumes that marketing works, that adspend is a given, that companies will always advertise. But what meaning do these assumptions have when the language of business doesn't agree?

THE DECLINING EFFECTIVENESS OF MASS ADVERTISING

We must accept the fact that there is no 'mass' in 'mass media' any more and leverage more targeted approaches.

Jim Stengel, Chief Marketing Officer, Procter & Gamble, AAAA 2004 Media Conference, 11 February 2004

The last decade has seen an explosion in media. Not only has the number of TV channels multiplied ad infinitum, but press launches and digital media have appeared on the scene too. The internet and mobile phones have become integral parts of many people's daily lives. DVDs have advanced on video technology, and computers have become leaner, meaner and fitter, and much cheaper than we could ever have imagined.

Video games offer virtual reality experiences and are becoming a more popular advertising medium: in May 2006, Microsoft reportedly paid $400 million for Massive Incorporated, a firm that specializes in placing ads in games. Toyota was the first advertiser to buy a 'dynamic billboard' from Massive in July 2006. It appeared in the game *Anarchy Online* and promoted the Yaris.

It is just 20 years since video recorders (VCRs) became standard boxes underneath televisions. Now VCRs are being ditched in favour of DVD players and personal video recorders (PVRs). In the United States, the PVR TiVo is in around 14 per cent of households, a figure that the Carmel Group estimates will to rise to 37 per cent in 2008.

While networks such as ABC are selling episodes of hit shows via the internet as part of a video-on-demand business model where advertising could subsidize the cost for consumers, some media owners and advertisers are experimenting with the really small screen. Fox has developed mobisodes, one-minute clips based on its hit show *24*, to be sent over mobile phones. Britain's ITV is planning to launch mobile clips of the perennial soap favourite *Coronation Street*. Meanwhile, NBC's Telemundo, a Spanish-language channel, is streaming *telenovelas* online, and Major League Baseball is selling games directly to viewers via its website, mlb.com.

Accenture predicts that, by 2011, interactive TV will be worth $5 billion a year, while Screen Digest estimates that, in Europe alone, there will be 8.7 million IPTV subscribers.

Measurement is increasingly challenging as media continue to fragment. Proving the effectiveness of a particular medium has become more complicated because the relationship between different media has become more complex.

The leaps and bounds made in technology offer advertisers more choice while at the same time making it harder for them to reach as *many* consumers via a campaign with terrestrial TV as its core component. Consumers are fickle, spending time with several media across an average day. They may still be watching programmes that were originally made for TV channels, but via a different method of distribution – through a digital connection or, as will increasingly be the case, through their computer or their mobile phone. The consultancy Informa suggests that there will be 125 million mobile TV customers by 2010, and services are already available on sophisticated handsets in hi-tech markets such as South Korea and Japan.

THE CHANGING CONSUMER

Technology – and particularly the internet – has empowered people by making information more accessible. This has made them more cynical about companies and savvier about advertising. A consumer can find out about a company's corporate social responsibility programme or information about more environmentally friendly consumer products from suppliers that don't have an advertising presence. Today's consumers increasingly want to feel good about their purchases and buy brands that reflect their ethical mores: sales of Fairtrade goods, for instance, rose in the UK by 40 per cent in 2005.

In the past, advertising was a major source of information for consumers seeking information about products and services. Today, people can decide for themselves whether they want to buy one brand over another; they wouldn't take too kindly to the patriarchal tone of early ads that made rash claims and blithe promises.

But one benefit for marketers of a world where choice proliferates is that, given the right incentives, consumers are more likely to be loyal;

they simply don't have time to consider each and every purchase week after week and are far more likely to stick with what they know. What's more, there is precious little time to waste. The average working week in the United States is 46 hours, with 38 per cent working for over 50 hours, while the Trades Union Congress estimates that Britons work 36 million hours of free overtime every year. This increase in working hours has put a huge strain on leisure time, so mass media find themselves competing not just with other media, but with other activities too.

Attention spans have shortened and we absorb information in bite-sized chunks. In the 1930s and 1940s, families huddled around a wireless set or went to the cinema to learn the day's news; today headlines can be zapped to mobile phones or scanned online in seconds. Sixty-second news shows and ticker-tape headlines on TV have become de rigueur. It's becoming much harder to track media consumption when a consumer can be online while flicking through a newspaper with the TV or radio on in the background. Who knows which particular medium has someone's attention at any one time?

One fact is certain. The day-after recall of television commercials has been in steady decline over the last 40 years. The publishing and consulting company Media Dynamics estimates in its publication *TV Dimensions* that, despite TV CPMs (cost per thousand viewers reached by the advertising) increasing by 68 per cent since 1995, TV ad recall fell in the United States from 40 per cent in 1960 to just 6 per cent in 2003. On the basis of these figures, TV spot advertising is eight times less effective in the 2000s than it was in the 1960s – and it's a much more costly route to market to boot.

Considering that it costs more money to reach fewer people, it's not surprising that mass marketing is sometimes regarded as a profligate waste of corporate funds in many boardrooms. Combine this with a reluctance on the part of marketers to introduce sound metrics to prove that marketing can drive shareholder value and suddenly its 'poor relation' reputation becomes easier to understand.

INCREASED PRESSURE ON CORPORATE PROFITABILITY

I cannot remember a time, in the 25 or so years I have been in the industry, when clients have been so focused on cost.

Martin Sorrell, CEO, WPP, annual report 2002

After the new millennium, how to grow became an obsession with companies. They began to realize that markets and sectors were maturing, and growth could no longer be taken for granted. Instead, as the world headed for a recession, growth became synonymous with cutbacks. The trends to merge, downsize, restructure and outsource all indicated that businesses were rationalizing to find more productive ways of competing. Shareholders started to wield more power than ever. Listed companies began to become increasingly obsessed with the next set of interim results and how they could demonstrate an improvement in their performance. Corporate scandals at behemoths like Enron and WorldCom in 2001 meant that shareholders wanted as much information as possible about the companies in their portfolios – and who could blame them?

Just as shareholders wanted to be sure about their investments, so did boards. The marketing budget suddenly came under unprecedented scrutiny and, for the first time, many firms started to think that it wasn't a bona fide part of the overall overheads of their business. In this climate of cost cutting and belt tightening, marketing started to be regarded as an extravagance rather than a serious business function that could create value.

As part of the rationalization process in many organizations, call centres and IT functions began to be outsourced or even offshored. Companies in mature markets such as the UK and the United States accounted for 70 per cent of the entire business process offshoring (BPO) market in 2003. Private equity investment in BPO ballooned, from $1.1 billion in 1997 to $24.2 billion in 2002. Corporations such as HSBC, Prudential and BT all took advantage of the significant cost benefits of offshoring, mostly heading for India.

Whispers began to circulate about how outsourcing certain aspects of the marketing function would help to lower costs. In WPP's 2002 annual report, the CEO, Sir Martin Sorrell, observed:

> One interesting recent development is the growing interest in outsourcing parts or all of the marketing function. Clearly this is an opportunity for us and is being driven by CEOs' focus on costs and their analysis of their own investment in marketing services. Instead of concentrating solely on amounts spent outside the organisation, closer examination is being made of amounts spent inside the company. In a number of areas, including advertising, direct marketing and research, there is considerable interest in what can be done in externalising costs.

Marketers began to find that they were under intense pressure to justify their performance. Many were not especially well equipped to do so.

GROWING PAINS

The mature ad markets of the United States and the UK – along with many mainland European markets – have also demonstrated much slower advertising growth. Since 2000, it is the economies in Asia, Central and Eastern Europe and Latin America that are showing the most impressive growth, so companies have been cutting their cloth accordingly.

According to predictions by ZenithOptimedia, Brazil, China, India, Indonesia and Russia will contribute almost a quarter of the total growth in global adspend forecast between 2005 and 2008 and, during that period, they will increase their share of the world ad market from 7 per cent to 10 per cent. Their fast-growing economies are quickly transforming these countries into some of the world's largest ad markets even while they are still growing. A large – and still expanding – middle class in these territories means that they offer massive potential to companies.

Another example of shifting sands has been the realization that corporate profitability has replaced consumer confidence as the macroeconomic metric that determines adspend. Around the turn of the new millennium a corporate-led downturn in advertising revenues had hit media companies, and those organizations that had been swept up in the dotcom and telecoms bubble towards the end of the 1990s started to exercise restraint when it came to deciding how much to spend on advertising. Corporate profitability tumbled towards the end of 2000, and adspend fell with it. According to ZenithOptimedia and the US Bureau of Economic Analysis, both hit a trough in 2001 when their year-on-year growth declined by over 5 per cent.

This had massive implications for media companies, which found themselves fighting over their clients' advertising budgets to stay afloat. Nothing could be taken for granted any more. Magazines closed and redundancies were made. Revenues at previously profitable TV companies fell. Caution became the watchword in markets that had once been bold.

The Marketing Expenditure Trends Report, written by Patrick Barwise and Alan Styler (2003) and published by the London Business School, shows that, between 2001 and 2004, in the world's biggest ad markets – the United States, Japan, the UK, Germany and France – only interactive marketing grew by a significant amount: 29.8 per cent. Other areas that demonstrated growth – albeit less impressive by comparison – included brand PR/sponsorship (6.8 per cent), direct marketing (4.6 per cent) and sales promotion (3.5 per cent). Over the same period, advertising in media grew by just 0.7 per cent.

THE IMPACT OF INTERACTIVITY

KPMG International and the Economist Intelligence Unit surveyed senior executives in global companies for a 2006 report entitled *Rethinking the Business Model*. A quarter of the respondents were CEOs, company presidents or managing directors, and 38 per cent cited new technology as an issue that would demand major revisions to their business model. From a marketing point of view, interactive media have grown in popularity because they can track response, behaviour and actual sales, as well as giving marketers the flexibility to tweak marketing communications in real time if an idea fails to deliver.

One need only look at the rise and rise of search advertising over the past few years to notice just how much advertisers are flocking to make the most of a medium that – at long last – offers no wastage. Search advertising is now the world's fastest-growing ad market. In the UK, according to figures from PricewaterhouseCoopers and the Internet Advertising Bureau, paid-for search marketing saw the biggest growth in 2005, up 78.8 per cent to £764.4 million. It was the biggest growth story in online advertising in 2005, which increased by 65.6 per cent to be worth £1.4 billion, giving it a share in the UK's adspend of 7.8 per cent. Pundits are confidently speculating that online adspend will break the £2 billion barrier in the UK in 2006.

In an era of engagement, the interactivity and personalization options offered by the internet are valuable marketing tools, particularly from a customer service point of view. Think of the personal recommendations based on last purchases made by Amazon.com – how often have these persuaded you to add an item on impulse to your shopping cart?

The internet also allows consumers to do their research at home before heading out to the high street. For the first time, a medium can brand, advertise, research, track and sell as well as encourage loyalty. No wonder its popularity has grown so rapidly.

As technology has improved, the internet has also been able to create experiences for customers such as games, competitions or coffee-break fun – an area that mobile phone operators such as Nokia have been keen to enter too. Burger King's subservient chicken viral in the United States allowed 12 million surfers to type in commands to a man dressed in a chicken suit to reinforce its 'have it your way' proposition. Such campaigns are relatively cheap and easy to produce and, once a few people have enjoyed it, they will forward it to the addresses in their inbox. This passes the baton to consumers to sustain a campaign's momentum. If they like the idea enough, they will, offering proof, if it were needed, that it's not about how big marketing budgets are, but what their resources are and how they deploy them to best engage and interact with audiences.

As well as becoming more popular with advertisers, the internet has had an impact on mainstream businesses too. If you want to buy a new car, for instance, you're unlikely to head to a particular dealership without conducting some preliminary research online.

Super internet brands such as Amazon, eBay, Google, YouTube and MySpace have become power brands in their own right and more are emerging all the time. Meanwhile, traditional retailers such as supermarkets and clothes stores are leveraging their popularity to great effect online.

Yet it was only a few years ago that the internet was being written off as an advertising medium as agencies tried desperately to fit old media logic into the new media environment. An endless stream of conferences focused on click-through rates and the effectiveness of banner advertising and what prices media owners could reasonably charge for particular-sized spots. By the same token, many internet practitioners refused to meet the marketers halfway.

It is difficult to remember the turf wars between digital and traditional media because the internet is no longer a new medium. Today, according to US statistics from Nielsen and Jupiter, 70 per cent of the 77 million US homes that have an internet connection are broadband; in the UK, the Office of National Statistics estimates that two-thirds of adults in the UK regularly access the internet. Such critical mass has made the internet an affordable and accountable medium for advertisers.

It has also amassed more respect inside organizations. Today, rather than the digital or e-commerce part of an enterprise being a separate division, it is viewed as an integral part of the core business. Intranets are used for internal communication between staff, while websites provide a public face for a company – and perhaps have an e-commerce function too. The technology and its potential are evolving all the time.

With wireless-enabled handsets being tipped as the next breakthrough in mobile communications, researching and purchasing products through our mobile phones cannot be far away.

THE IMPLICATIONS

To face this challenging new world, marketers must change their ways, if they haven't already. At the moment, the marketing department simply isn't close enough to the centre of executive management of many businesses.

This is reflected in the results of Accenture's (2004) *High Performance Workforce Study, 2002–2003*, which shows the declining regard in which marketing is held.

Out of 200 executives at companies all over the world, just 23 per cent said that marketing makes a contribution of a very significant value compared with 61 per cent for sales and 43 per cent for customer service. Only 21 per cent ranked marketing as one of their organization's three most important functions.

Even among these 'converts', there were doubters. Only 28 per cent believed that the marketing function in their company performed better than the marketing functions at other companies within their industry.

And marketers' lack of staying power hasn't helped matters. A 2004 report by the executive search firm Spencer Stuart, *CMO Tenure: Slowing down the revolving door*, which surveyed the Top 100 branded companies showed that the average tenure of a chief marketing officer in the United States was 22.9 months, less than half that of the CEO's 53.8 months.

Given their propensity for itchy feet, it's unsurprising that so few marketers become CEOs. A survey by the Chartered Institute of Marketing (CIM) in the UK in 2005 found that only 11 FTSE 100 companies had a marketing director on their boards. The 11 companies were: BP (which has two), building services firm BPB, British Airways, Imperial Tobacco, Legal & General, Marks & Spencer, Morrisons, Rentokil Initial, SABMiller, Vodafone and Tesco.

With minimal board representation and little in the way of concrete evidence to demonstrate that they are helping to generate value, it's not difficult to see why many marketers move on. On the face of it, a new organization may offer a marketer the chance to launch a product or be involved with a big-budget campaign. But there's also the chance that it might set realistic and achievable expectations of the marketing function.

And for this to happen in a significant number of companies, the ad and media industries that service the marketing function need to consider the benefits of reinventing themselves. They frequently find themselves batting off accusations of being out-of-touch partners that have steadfastly refused to move with the times.

The Finance and Systems Director at Toyota Great Britain, Andrew Singer, is one such critic. He says: 'If David Ogilvy turned up in an ad agency today, he could take off his jacket and get straight back to work. They are the most old-fashioned and anachronistic businesses. They are resistant to change and fear it for all the wrong reasons.'

To play a part in making their clients more successful, agencies have to start by understanding the business challenges faced by their clients. Once they show signs of caring about the same things as their clients – particularly in terms of generating value – they will find themselves back in favour.

In turn, agencies should realign themselves so they are not just about the creative work but also about business. If they sold the benefits of advertising to their clients and showed how it could generate value while at the same time offering more impartial advice to their clients, they would be held in higher esteem in the boardroom.

Agencies could be instrumental in helping companies to develop an ROI-led approach to marketing, where it is prioritized, well organized and structured. Metrics and evaluation need to come to the forefront rather than being a permanent fixture on agencies' and marketing directors' 'to-do' lists. And, internally, chief executives and chief financial officers need to get closer to the marketing process and understand the best approach for it to generate significant returns.

WHAT THIS BOOK SETS OUT TO DO

A handful of organizations have already demonstrated that an investment-led approach to marketing communication can make a huge impact on the financial performance of a company. In this book, we single out and consistently champion the achievements of four companies. They demonstrate a more considered, business-oriented approach to their marketing strategies and have consequently enjoyed an impressive financial and business performance:

- *Procter & Gamble* under the leadership of AG Lafley, who started with the company as an assistant brand manager on Tide, embarked

on a strategy of focusing on its big global brands supported by innovation in products and marketing. Today, P&G has 22 billion-dollar
brands versus 10 in 2000. Between 2002 and 2006, it grew sales at
twice the rate of its peers and doubled its annual profits.

- *Toyota*'s marketing of its main marque as well as its Lexus brand has
  helped it to grow its stock market value to 15 times that of General
  Motors. It now has a 15 per cent market share of the global car
  market and is well on the way to eclipsing GM, the world's biggest
  car manufacturer.

- *O2*, the mobile phone operator, was sold to the Spanish telecom
  Telefonica for £17.7 billion in 2005. Just four years before the sale, it
  had been flailing as BT Cellnet. O2's value was boosted by the
  creation of a memorable brand and a customer-centric proposition.

- *British Airways* has always understood the power of marketing and
  what it can achieve. Following the 2001 terrorist attacks and a glut of
  low-cost airlines threatening to erode its customer base, BA rose
  from the ashes. It once again became one of the world's most profitable airlines, partly on account of a sustained investment in
  marketing that helped to reposition it.

Marrying ROI with creativity and brands can multiply marketing's
potency. To assess how powerful an idea is, ROI metrics need to be
created and tested, but companies also need to organize themselves to
maximize marketing's payback. New models for marketing communications are being deployed not only to engage more elusive consumers,
but also to deliver more fiscal accountability required from boards.

And not a moment too soon either.

2

A change in philosophy

WHAT IS MARKETING ROI?

Without the right measurement, we really don't know how well our efforts work. We don't really know if we're in touch with our consumers. This is a $450 billion industry and we're making decisions with less data and discipline than we apply to $100,000 decisions in other aspects of our businesses. We lack an industry standard for measurement. We need a method to determine the effectiveness of our efforts.

> Jim Stengel, Chief Marketing Officer, Procter & Gamble,
> 'Staying in touch with the consumer', AAAA Conference,
> 12 February 2004

Eighteen months after making this speech, Jim Stengel addressed the Association of National Advertisers (ANA) Conference in the United States in October 2005. He shared with the audience the mission of P&G marketers:

- Live our corporate purpose of 'Touching Lives and Improving Life' through our brands and through our marketing.
- Have a greater and more personal understanding of the consumers we serve.

- Lead the industry to better meet the needs of consumers, developing better measurement tools for ROI and new ways to market in more consumer-centric ways.
- To be the best, most inspired, brand-building marketing organization in the world.

Stengel, who has been part of P&G's dramatic business transformation under chairman and chief executive AG Lafley (see Chapter 3), is proof that ROI is not about marketing by numbers. Within P&G, ROI is about identifying and implementing measurement tools that can demonstrate marketing's power to create, inspire and influence human behaviour.

ROI is regarded within the organization as being as important as understanding the consumers that P&G seeks to attract. After putting ROI at the heart of its mission, P&G has never looked back.

Bernhard Glock, P&G's manager of global media and communication since September 2003, comments: 'If you have an ROI mindset – in other words, a mindset of getting most value out of every dollar spent, for the consumer and the company – and you combine mining and digging into consumer insights with the rigorous application of sophisticated tools and approaches, ROI becomes much more than wishful thinking.'

Defining Marketing ROI

Marketing return on investment (ROI) is about creating positive value for a business or brand through demonstrating cost versus payback. A lot of marketing is currently well skilled in demonstrating effect, yet fails miserably when it comes to demonstrating actual cost-effectiveness.

A process that can deliver profitable marketing communication needs to involve a clear line of sight between communication and business result. It also needs to define the short (within 6–8 weeks), medium (2–12 months) and long term (over 12 months), as well as clearly establishing what the 'R' in ROI stands for. The return on investment will differ according to the brand and its objective. But it will always need to be a metric that is readable and attributable to a business metric. What's more, it will need to demonstrate relative cost-effectiveness versus other alternatives.

To achieve this, usable data are essential. Frank Harrison, Strategic Resources Director for ZenithOptimedia Worldwide, says: 'If you only have data on mass media, you will tend to repeat your best TV or print activity. You'll never think to do more point-of-sale activity because you'll never have good enough data to show how effective an in-store display was.'

Ditching the jargon

Part of the problem with ROI is that the industry gets tangled up in its own terminology. Take a look at this definition of ROI by Hunter Hastings, the managing partner of MMI Consulting Group:

> Total ROI evaluates the efficiency of the total marketing budget: (A) What is the value (in increased net sales revenue and brand gross margin) of bonding consumers more closely to the brand (e.g. creating trial, translating trial into repeat purchase and translating repeat purchase into loyalty). This can be thought of as a continuum of brand involvement; and (B) What is the cost in marketing expenditures to move those consumers up the continuum? 'A' divided by 'B' is total Marketing ROI.

Congratulations if you managed to reach the end without your attention tailing off. Without wishing to be too harsh on Hastings, this technical definition is long-winded, dry and confusing. It typifies definitions of ROI that make it seem inaccessible and impossible to achieve – like an elusive equation that can only be cracked by boffins in white coats armed with special computers.

For ROI to be easy to achieve, a new mindset is required that uses a lexicon that simplifies rather than bewilders. The following are suggestions to make it a more straightforward science:

1. *Think of Marketing ROI as another name for 'profit'.* Thinking of Marketing ROI as 'profit' helps to re-frame thinking around the subject. Marketing is the skill of evaluating and managing company resources: people, time and money. Marketing's objective should be to deliver a profit back to the company for the purposes of those investments.

    There are two types of profit: improved cash flow – positive sales lifts in the short term; and appreciated value of an asset – the long-term sales effect that happens as a result of the marketing investment.
2. *Treat the marketing budget as a 'loan'.* Forget the word 'budget'; that implies money that will be spent without any sign of a return. Instead, let's treat the marketing budget as a loan that a marketer needs to pay back with interest.

If that loan were invested in a bank, it would reap 3 or 4 per cent interest. Marketing needs to perform better to secure that loan. Marketing doesn't have the luxury, as a mortgage does, of a 25-year term, so profit needs to be evaluated over time or the investment horizon.

On receipt of this 'loan', evaluate your potential for profit and assess the risk of marketing versus other potential investment options. Looking at the broader picture, ask yourself honestly if that money would generate a better return if it were to be invested elsewhere. These are the investment trade-offs a board is looking to make with corporate funds. If marketers can regard their loans more objectively – as opposed to always believing that marketing is the answer – their colleagues in the boardroom will demonstrate greater respect for their judgement.

3. *Consider marketing services companies as your 'stockbrokers'.* Good stockbrokers can potentially make you a lot of money, so it can pay to be in constant dialogue with them. Remunerate them appropriately for their services. If you think you don't need their advice, don't pay for it; an online trading account will help you to buy and sell shares for a much lower fee, but you will have to do the investing on your own. In the end, it is a combination of the right advice and your own judgement that creates the difference between making a profit and sustaining a loss in marketing.

    Stockbrokers are employed for their expertise and experience – they are always playing the markets. They have seen clients win and lose money. They will do the homework on the consumer and provide advice on your behalf. Traditionally, they have been paid on a commission or a fee based on costs. While this has served marketers well, there is a growing focus on more accountable approaches to remuneration that incentivizes Marketing ROI. For example, if you give agencies a share of your profits, the chances are they are more likely to perform; it's human nature. Agencies will pull out all the stops if their pay packet pivots on their performance.

    Some market-leading advertisers are picking up on this concept and are starting to implement remuneration structures that ditch the fee-based system in favour of performance-related pay. P&G, for instance, remunerates its ad agencies on a percentage of sales on a global level. The consumer packaged goods Goliath focuses its agencies on growth and the bigger global picture. Toyota, too, incentivizes its media agencies for improving media effectiveness and growing brand measures.

To work effectively for you, agencies need careful management. If you manage them well, you will enjoy more benefits from the relationship. In the long term, this means that your agencies will help your business performance.

Just like stockbrokers, different agencies will adopt different strategies; there's no 'one size fits all' approach. This is why it's important to judge agencies on their results – on how they have helped to grow their client's businesses – rather than on the route they took to get there. Take time to make an informed decision when being advised by marketing 'stockbrokers'. The investment choices that you settle on for your loan are your responsibility; the buck stops with you, not your agencies.

4. *Think of marketing channels as different 'ways of making money'.* For marketers managing loans, different types of investment work in a variety of ways to generate a return. Here are three examples of marketing channels and their investment equivalents:
   - Large-scale television brand campaigns are the marketing investor's equivalent to buying a house. There is a need to take out a mortgage with significant up-front costs and therefore there are bigger risks involved. Just as with buying a house, it is tempting to become wrapped up emotionally in the aesthetics and design minutiae rather than the foundations. For many, the prospect of buying a house presents the best long-term investment decision they ever make. The same could be said of marketers and large-scale TV brand campaigns.
   - Direct response and direct marketing are short-term deposits that generate low-risk but more consistent short-term profits.
   - Trade and consumer promotions provide wins in the short term, but little in the way of sustainable returns.

Marketers face a relentless juggling act to keep all these different balls in the air at any one time.

Creativity plays a crucial role here because the execution itself can be as important as the strategy; eg direct marketing might be the right channel, but a poor execution could make it the wrong investment. What's the point in spending all that time figuring out a watertight strategy if a drab mail-out means it is instantly chucked in the bin? And, just as with buying a house where everything needs attention, unremarkable creative work that fails to grab the attention of TV viewers will turn a brand campaign into a money pit, making it a poor investment choice in the long term.

STUDYING THE MARKET

Speak to anyone who has experience of investing in stocks and shares and they will confirm that, for every share tip that paid out handsomely, there were just as many that failed to perform, or even resulted in a disastrous loss.

Similarly, in marketing, for every Whassup – a campaign that helped lift sales of Budweiser by 50 per cent in the United States – there are hundreds of campaigns that haven't worked.

Keep tabs on what works and study effectiveness: do your homework and compile dossiers of successful campaigns. Why is a particular campaign driving product sales? What do successful campaigns have in common? Can you spot the similarities between brands in specific sectors? Is what makes a Honda campaign effective the same for Toyota or Volkswagen? If not, what makes it different? Develop your own thoughts and theories, and have opinions on campaigns that are said to be 'working'. What makes them work?

Market-mix modelling, post evaluation and tracking cause and effect can help you to maximize your Marketing ROI and will strengthen the case for marketing in the boardroom. But when you present your ideas to non-marketing peers in your organization, it is also useful if you can demonstrate a solid understanding of what constitutes a successful campaign. Champion those marketing communications that you regard as blazing an exemplary trail.

WHY MARKETING ROI IS DIFFICULT TO ACHIEVE

The hurdles faced by marketers

Every year, senior marketers board the *Aurora* for a three-day marketing forum. We attended the forum in 2004 and spoke to a group of 40 marketers from organizations as diverse as PricewaterhouseCoopers, Toyota and Kimberly-Clark about their views on ROI and its role within marketing. They were passionate about the subject and wanted to make their marketing decisions more accountable. Yet they faced considerable challenges in trying to place ROI at the heart of their marketing operations.

Compounding these challenges, marketers faced a number of issues in implementing ROI.

A dearth of data

The challenge…

Marketers' frustration with poor-quality data was a near-universal sentiment. It meant that they were falling down at the first fence when trying to justify performance and prove a return to their colleagues. Without proper metrics in place, some of these businesses had to use ROI key performance indicators (KPIs) on the basis that they were the right criteria because they were easy to measure. In other cases, brand awareness or media value was a popular metric. Again, both fall a long way short of measuring actual value.

Common problems…

An obsession with metrics can lead to marketers making the wrong marketing choices. For instance, advertisers are drawn towards TV because it is straightforward to measure. Yet ease of measurement doesn't automatically make it the *right* medium for a particular message.

In some organizations, the spotlight on metrics can be so intense that marketers can find themselves using the wrong ones. The logic here is that at least they're measuring *something*. A more sophisticated approach is required that doesn't just concern itself with measuring the size of audiences, but instead measures the effects that the advertising is having on audiences. In other words, the emphasis should be firmly focused on the *quality* rather than quantity of audiences.

Too much data, too little time

The challenge…

Marketing departments have been culled in many organizations, resulting in fewer people and less expertise devoted to marketing activity post-mortems. Yet the marketers agreed that one of the only ways they could learn for the future was to assess past activity. Regardless of whether or not a particular marketing activity was successful, past advertising can help to establish benchmarks and can help build a framework of realistic objectives and expectations.

Common problems…

In large organizations, the KPIs of different marketing communications bear no relation to each other. For instance, direct marketing mail-outs focus on cost per sell whereas brand advertising is more concerned with brand preference. Media measurement is all about reach and frequency, while PR is busy counting column inches and assessing whether they are positive or negative. Considering all of the options open to marketers, it's becoming increasingly difficult for them to manage an ever fatter portfolio of marketing challenges and to feel confident that they are making informed investment decisions.

The marketer's role has become more about planning the next campaign and less about assessing former activity. This is when marketing starts to look more and more like a game of chance and less and less like an informed strategy that links back to business objectives and driving value.

They just don't understand me

The challenge…

Finance directors sometimes suffer from a serious knowledge gap in their grasp of marketing issues. If they can't see a sales uplift, they disregard the potential contribution that can be made by marketing. This means that aspects of value generation, such as brand value, are not regarded as acceptable uses of resource in their opinion.

Common problems…

At the same time, marketers need to use the language of finance to sell the case for marketing, but often they're just not built this way. Marketers, after all, pursued a career in marketing because they didn't want to be accountants; hence there is a widespread lack of confidence in their ability to 'speak finance'.

Marketing budget recommendations and allocation decisions are often driven by marketing communications managers who are histori-cally not particularly well versed in the rigours of financial or statistical training. These managers also tend to be less practised in strategic processes such as Six Sigma, strategy maps and balanced scorecards that form an integral part of everyday life in other departments.

Despite concepts such as net present value, risk hurdle rates and ROI being available to marketers, only a handful have been able to adapt them to make them relevant to marketing. The need for marketing to adapt to the changing world is matched by a need for marketers to change and to become more disciplined in their understanding of these processes and how they can assist them in more rigorous decision making. Perhaps then marketing will rise up the food chain. Currently, it's unsurprising to learn that CEOs are nearly four times more likely to be from a finance background than a marketing one.

Long- versus short-term benefit

The challenge...

Brands need time to be built. Frank Harrison compares the investment required for the brand-building process to the flight of a jumbo jet:

> It costs an enormous amount of money to launch a brand. If you get it high enough off the ground so that sales rocket and it enjoys double-digit growth, it can become a market leader and you can maintain your market leadership position at a reduced cost per sale. But if you stop your advertising, it's disastrous. It's like a jumbo jet, which uses 80 per cent of its fuel taking off and landing. Once it starts going down, it takes a lot to pull it back again. Similarly, if you cut marketing expenditure and stop advertising, in the short term you'll make a great big profit, but it will take a great deal of investment to pull the brand back up to its previous market share.

Harrison illustrates his point with the example of Heinz. An iconic advertiser in the 1970s and 1980s – most memorably, showing a young Margaret Thatcher tucking into a plateful of baked beans in 1988 – Heinz diverted its spend away from TV and into direct mail in the 1980s. The result? Loss of market share.

Common problems...

Marketers encounter problems in trying to justify long-term marketing efforts in a corporate environment obsessed by 90-day reporting periods. The challenge is that, while it is easier to measure the short-term effect, marketers have struggled to quantify the long-term effect. Meanwhile, boards have been unwilling to account for it. Even products such as cars, which have long purchase cycles, tend to be more focused on monthly vehicle sales results rather than measuring the lifetime value of a new customer.

Organizational structural problems

The challenge...

In larger marketing organizations, business units are focused on sales in their particular market and are less interested in 'the brand'. In such organizations, marketing can often find itself stuck in a silo where it locks horns with sales.

Common problems...

Fiefdoms occur, and some marketers admit that they do little to break them down. Marketers concentrate on achieving their own personal targets rather than being aware of the bigger, corporate picture. In such an environment, marketers' ambition becomes focused on growing and defending the marketing budget rather than how they can best achieve profitability.

New media

The challenge...

Marketers complain that there is a lack of effective research that can prove the case for new communication channels. This, they claim, hampers their ability to embrace new channels, so they stick with what's familiar, especially television, deeming it 'safer'.

Common problems...

It remains a challenge to find ways to measure certain 'new' channels, and even metrics for 'old' media are far from perfect.

Agency neutrality

The challenge...

Marketers commented on agencies' reluctance to recommend channels beyond their own areas of expertise, including non-mainstream channels. They lamented agencies' lack of ability to evaluate the value of brand advertising as opposed to channels that are predisposed towards measurement, such as the internet and direct marketing. They particularly commented on the lack of focus on ROI within ad agencies.

Common problems…

Since the marketing services industry has fragmented, a 'full service' is rarely able to be delivered in-house by a single agency. A typical agency is simply not structured to provide specialist expertise across different communication disciplines, meaning that generalists who are actually genuine are thin on the ground.

Agencies are unlikely to be solutions-neutral because their natural tendency is to sell the service with which they are most comfortable. Equally, very few marketers are willing to pay for integration strategies, preferring to pay their agencies for implementation instead.

Expectations of marketing's role

The challenge…

Marketers agreed that advertising effectiveness needed to be backed up by hard evidence if marketing was to be made a more credible part of their operations. Yet they were nervous about the risks involved. For example, some feared that they would fail to live up to the high expectations imposed on the marketing function within their organizations.

Common problems…

Business targets in general are more aggressive than ever, and growth is harder for corporations to come by. According to a survey by the management consultants Bain & Company, two-thirds of senior executives believe that growth is much harder to achieve today than it was five years ago, and they are feeling the heat: the average company sets revenue targets at more than two times its market growth rate, with earnings targets four times as high.

It's no wonder that marketers feel pressured when their targets are nigh on impossible to achieve. Couple this with one of the most popular ways to reduce costs and maintain margins – slashing the marketing budget – and it's easy to see how disillusionment with marketing itself has crept in.

The hurdles faced by marketing directors and CEOs

Another reason why ROI is difficult to achieve is the often elusive relationship between marketing and financial return. Compared with that of other departments, marketing spend is difficult to evaluate against a fixed-cost item. It's generally much easier to see how an upgraded IT system, a sales promotion or a staff-training programme delivers a return because it lends itself to a straightforward 'before and after' analysis.

Ingrid Murray, Managing Director at Ninah Consulting, which formed in 1997 to help justify the value of marketing, illustrates this point:

> Imagine you're a managing director and, on one side, your marketing director is saying 'I want £3 million for my new ad campaign but I'm not sure it will deliver.' On the other side, you've got a sales director saying 'We've evaluated these promotions and we know that the sales uplift is 30 per cent.' What are you going to decide? It's obvious… unless you have a mechanism which can prove the brand-building aspect of the advertising.

If a marketing director had some means of demonstrating how that £3 million ad campaign could transform a £60 million brand into one worth £70 million, it would be a different story.

A protective and territorial style of managing individual departments aggravates matters. Stronger top-down leadership could certainly improve internal communication to minimize the turf wars between departments and unite them towards common corporate goals. Murray says: 'A significant portion of the work we get is from silos that are created by an organization's size, culture or politics. When we run workshops for sales, marketing and finance staff, they often have to be introduced because they don't normally work with each other.'

The time lag between marketing investment and return can also marginalize marketing when budgets are being allocated. A sales director can show short-term sales uplift – a tempting proposition when the next set of interim results is fast approaching. The marketing director, however, should be interested in value generation over the next three years. That value will take time to filter back into the business. Marketers must make a compelling case to convince their colleagues that the value generated by marketing activity can positively contribute to the long-term financial health of the organization.

The short tenures of marketing directors are also not synonymous with a culture of consistency.

What's more, many marketing directors fail to employ the very analytics that would help them to articulate the case for marketing. Consequently, they fall into the trap of unveiling a marketing strategy that is still based around cost rather than value generation and weakens it right from the start. The result? The sales director gets more cash while marketing's reputation continues to suffer.

Many marketers might insist that what they do is 'creative', so it is impossible to measure in terms of hard data. But, in an accountable world, creativity can't be used as a 'get out of jail free' card. Murray says: 'It's better to be creative knowing that your creativity is focused for strongest impact and is really driving performance.'

What's more, the value of creativity permeates modern business culture; it's not confined to the marketing department. Julian Elliott, the Head of Group Marketing Effectiveness at Lloyds TSB, comments: 'There is a presumption that marketing can't be measure or proved, and I just don't think that's the case. Marketing does have some gems of ideas, inspiration and blue-sky moments, but those are also happening in software engineering.'

HOW SHOULD MARKETERS RESPOND?

By applying the fundamentals of investment management to their business, marketers can gain credibility. What's more, by talking about 'value' rather than 'cost', they will instantly earn themselves more respect among their colleagues.

For instance, if a direct marketing programme costing £10 million could generate a return of 300 per cent, it should be regarded as £30 million of value rather than £10 million of cost. Even if the marketing activity did not generate such an impressive return, the cost of a campaign should always be deducted from ROI – any figures should always subtract the cost of the initial investment.

If you were buying stocks and shares you would deduct their original purchase price when working out the return they had delivered. The same applies to the return on a marketing investment. In this way, marketers can consider presenting themselves as investment managers. By using financial terms and applying rigorous analytical tools to back up their proposed strategies, they will be taken more seriously. Robust financial arguments lead to decision making within organizations. Woolly data and unreliable metrics lead nowhere.

Marketing-mix and Marketing ROI systems are not new-fangled inventions, but many marketers simply haven't got into the habit of integrating them into their way of working. A 2003 *Reveries* survey of marketing directors showed that 72 per cent felt that they lacked the data to assess the return of their marketing investments. Sixteen per cent used sales data, while 22 per cent used research such as focus groups, benchmarking, syndicated sales data analysis and brand awareness studies.

True, Marketing ROI could benefit from becoming more sophisticated in its analyses; marketing-mix models have yet to find a way of showing the influence of different media on each other. It's still a challenge to prove how a TV branding campaign boosts the response of a direct mail push, for example.

In a stable market environment, these models work well. But when advertisers are confronting more serious challenges, they are required to perform harder. Some would also argue that it is during such periods that a strong marketing strategy is key. John Sills, Chief Financial Officer at Orange Broadband, observes: 'Marketers would sooner spend lots of money if the message is good because it proves that advertising works. But the times when I release more money are when we need to sustain our performance.'

Marketers' judgement is still needed, and here their unparalleled knowledge about consumers comes to the fore. This doesn't simply entail collecting insight on a particular product any more; it involves developing an understanding of how consumers prefer to be targeted.

Bernhard Glock at P&G says: 'We focus on connecting with consumers in terms of when and where they are receptive to our messages. This extends far beyond old-fashioned consumer insights; it's more about being relevant to the consumer so we are welcomed on their terms. This makes our messages much more effective.'

Consumers are complex creatures who can't be relied on to follow the rules. Marketers need to be responsive, and be completely unafraid of venturing off-piste when things don't go according to plan.

Invest in investing

The development of ROI measures requires a substantial commitment to data gathering and analysis. Most practitioners of sophisticated Marketing ROI business practices employ consultants or internal staff familiar with modelling techniques and finance. Unless a company has an extensive data-gathering and analytics capability, getting started needs a substantial upfront investment and some new skill-sets. It requires top management commitment, and a commitment to the long-term view.

Institutionalizing ROI

More enlightened marketers are starting to grasp the nettle and embrace the changes required to make their decisions more accountable. In the United States, the ANA sponsored a study that was published in *Advertising Age* on 13 October 2003. In the survey, 70 per cent of marketing executives agreed with the statement that ROI represented a long-term change in how they did business. Accepting that change is inevitable is an important first step.

Consequently, a year-long ANA marketing accountability task force compiled best practice guidelines in October 2005, which recommended the following:

- Create a culture of accountability. This requires:
  - a top-down endorsed approach;
  - an inclusive, repeatable process;
  - a method that provides employees with confidence for both its numerical accuracy and its perceived value and comparability.
- Employ unique metrics that reflect management expectations.
- Produce a rigorous, end-to-end process to deliver superior marketing results.
- Embrace the responsibility for short-term ROI of expenditures and go beyond to demand accountability for nurturing brand equity.

It's important to remember that a change in philosophy does not solely pivot on introducing more reliable metrics. Kevin Clancy and Randy Stone make this point in their *Harvard Business Review* article from June 2005, 'Don't blame the metrics'. They argue that the numbers are just a means to an end; a more holistic attitude to improving marketing performance is required, of which ROI is just one aspect. They write:

> Marketers aren't unhappy because they can't measure marketing performance. They're unhappy because they now can – and they don't like what they see. They need to go beyond metrics and take a hard look at why the numbers are so bad: their marketing strategies are often flawed and their spending is inefficient. With increasing precision, they're measuring the impact of ill-defined targeting, weak positioning, mediocre advertising, pedestrian products and services, giveaway promotions, and poorly allocated spending.

They add: 'Measuring marketing ROI won't improve performance. Fixing broken strategy and optimizing the marketing budget will.'

3

Our Marketing ROI stars:
Learning from signature marketers

Start-ups that launched on a shoestring and became success stories captivate the business community.

In 1995, for instance, Jeff Bezos started selling books that were shipped from a garage in Seattle. Today, Bezos is the chief executive of Amazon.com, the byword for books online. In the last decade, Amazon.com has built up a network of over 20 fulfilment centres around the world and operates local e-commerce sites in the UK, Germany, Japan, France, Canada and China.

Despite the significant number of headlines and column inches that they attract, examples such as Amazon.com – which show that entrepreneurial energy can flout convention and change consumer behaviour – are few and far between. Start-ups can afford to eschew a traditional approach and follow a more daring path because – at the beginning at least – they have nothing to lose.

Yet the majority of marketers work in structured business environments operating in mature sectors where established brands sell to consumers through conventional distribution channels. They have a clearly defined competitive set and certain targets to meet, and accountability is not an optional extra. Achieving stand-out where there is a rigid rule book to follow is a considerable accomplishment. Success under these circumstances is particularly worthy of praise.

Our criteria for selecting and celebrating this particular batch of Marketing ROI stars are as follows:

- Ability to compete in mature sectors where they have stood out for all the right reasons and where marketing has been one of the lead success criteria.
- Ability to turn around a major business problem or reinvigorate the business through marketing communication. They demonstrate that marketing was a central part of the business strategy and resultant success.
- Clear demonstration of financial performance in terms of increased shareholder value as well as traditional marketing criteria for success. None of the examples include a successful launch at a time when the overall health of the company has been poor. Conversely, none of our Marketing ROI stars show that the advertising worked despite the product offering being completely wrong.

In this chapter, we will describe how Toyota, Procter & Gamble, O2 and British Airways met specific Marketing ROI challenges. We will examine how they approached the development of their marketing and implemented processes to help them achieve their targets – and much more.

We refer to our Marketing ROI stars in the chapters that follow, continuing to point out ways in which they show what a powerful investment choice marketing can be.

TOYOTA MOTOR CORPORATION: DRIVING IN TOP GEAR

Background

Toyota's chairman, Hiroshi Okuda, wants Toyota to have a 15 per cent share of the global car market. His plans to eclipse General Motors as the market leader look ever more achievable by the day.

In the fiscal year 2005–06, Toyota made $12.1 billion in profits. Its stock market value is now 15 times that of General Motors, and its eco-friendly Prius, which uses hybrid technology, has made it a pioneer in the car industry for being serious about reducing carbon emissions.

Meanwhile its Corolla model, launched in 1996, is one of the best-selling cars of all time: 30 million Corollas have been made in the last 10 years.

Toyota's upmarket Lexus marque has enjoyed extraordinary growth. In 1991, just three years after it had unveiled its first-ever vehicle at auto shows around the world, Lexus had become the best-selling import in the United States, outperforming Mercedes and BMW, with sales of 70,000 a year. Growth continued to balloon: nine years later in 2000, it had become the best-selling luxury nameplate in the United States. Lexus is now beginning to gather momentum in Europe too.

And the Scion, Toyota's compact range targeting a youth market in the United States, was launched in 2004 as a means of targeting Generation Y, in other words the kids of the baby boomers who have helped Toyota to grow its market share so rapidly. Since its introduction, Toyota has invested in non-traditional advertising to market it to young drivers, sponsoring events at nightclubs and selling DJ bags and snowboard jackets on its website. The strategy has paid off: the average age of a Scion buyer is 31, the youngest in the US car industry. This bodes well for Toyota, which has one of the highest loyalties of all of the car manufacturers.

When it sought to target the same group in Europe, Toyota toyed with the idea of launching the Scion brand, but instead decided to downplay Toyota and flag up the name of the car itself, Aygo. Below we use the Aygo example to highlight Toyota's innovative approach to marketing, which helped the car to achieve considerable stand-out and contributed to improving Toyota's business success.

Challenge

The Peugeot 107, Citroën C1 and Toyota Aygo are three different badges for the same economical car aimed at younger drivers following a joint venture established by Toyota and PSA Peugeot Citroën. The three car manufacturers wanted to produce a small car that shared the technology required to reduce CO_2 emissions.

All three cars were produced at the same factory in the Czech Republic, and have the same chassis and engine.

Because the three are essentially the same vehicle, the Aygo's marketing had to play an integral part in prompting decision making and shifting sales because there was no discernible difference between the three products and their performance on the road. Timing was another factor: the three vehicles were all launching in the same month.

Toyota had to step up its marketing effort to improve its credentials among younger European drivers. As Toyota's reputation was firmly built around reliability, it was a beacon brand for older drivers, presenting it with a real marketing challenge. As Martin Czerwinski, the Supervisor Media and Creative Strategy at ZenithOptimedia in Germany (the agency that worked with Toyota on the Aygo launch), points out: 'It's really difficult to become a "cool" brand: 80 per cent of brands that try it don't make it.'

The communication objectives for the campaign were:

- to create awareness and enquiry among and attract young buyers;
- to create customers who offer Toyota strong potential in the lifetime value stakes;
- to communicate a young and stylish image for the Aygo by triggering buzz and intrigue around the new car.

The metrics that were introduced to gauge the campaign's success included:

- sales;
- cost per unit (based on communication budget/sales);
- effective sales price (including specials like MP3 players).

Solution

The Aygo audience across Europe was identified as optimistic, confident, clever and creative urbanites, so Toyota engaged with them via the 'urban playground', a pop culture network comprising bars, clubs, concerts and cinemas in town and city centres. Music was a central plank in the Aygo armoury. A central website, Aygo.com, was adapted for local market usage following the vehicle's launch, which was backed up with the invitation to 'do something memorable'.

Online, Aygo used blogs, instant messenger, podcasts and home page sponsorships as well as its own websites. E-mail and mobile activity, gaming, screen savers and videos helped the brand to build a dialogue with the target group. Online also played a key part in data capture.

Aygo had its own quarterly lifestyle magazine, which was written to appeal to tastes across Europe. The Aygo magazine drove even more traffic online.

The campaign was pan-European with a centrally led media strategy. However, particular emphasis was placed on two markets: Germany and the UK.

Germany

In Germany, the positioning was 'Lust auf morgen', which translates as 'looking forward for tomorrow'. Aygo teamed up with German hip-hop group The Fantastic Four on cross-media activity that included a partnership with MTV, city events, radio and club promotions.

Early buzz was created when, in Germany, a website called Aygo.de launched with no reference to Toyota. This was a deliberate strategy on the part of Toyota and ZenithOptimedia because, as Czerwinski points out: 'Toyota was not a desirable brand with the younger target market; it was uncool. We had to rejuvenate it.'

By the time it became clear that the site was linked to Toyota, the Aygo's credibility had already been established, banishing any lingering negative preconceptions of the Toyota brand among the target group.

UK

In the UK, a spoof record launch – a track called 'Do something memorable' – heralded the Aygo's arrival. The Aygo logo appeared on posters and ads in the music and entertainment press, directing consumers to the URL. Aygo subsequently sponsored TV content such as the Channel 4 music concert, T4 On The Beach, and had a presence at major UK festivals as well as sponsoring Yahoo Music's summer festival guide.

Just as in Germany, references to Toyota were kept low-key: a third of the UK launch budget was spent without reference to Toyota or any mention of the new car.

Traditionally, approximately 90 per cent of the media budget on a car launch is dominated by press, TV and outdoor, but this time half was spent on events, online and cinema and radio. Events, in particular, were vital in establishing word of mouth, generating buzz and providing a brand experience.

Results

The spoof record launch in the UK helped to increase traffic sixfold to the Aygo website. Brochure requests were seven times higher than those for the previous major Toyota launches in the UK, and 70 per cent of requests came from consumers under 40 – a significantly younger crowd than Toyota was traditionally accustomed to: for other Toyota vehicles, over two-thirds of brochure requests tend to come from the over-40s.

Most impressively, in Germany, sales of the Aygo were significantly higher than for the Peugeot 107 and the Citroën C1 combined – a trend that, it is believed, was replicated across other key European markets. Between January and September 2005, the cost per unit sold was €700 for the Aygo, €1,315 for the Peugeot 107 and €4,887 for the Citroën C1, meaning that Toyota sold more cars at under a quarter of the average marketing cost per unit. What's more, establishing the Aygo as a youth brand had been a hit: the average age of an Aygo driver was 30 – the youngest in Germany's car market.

This integrated campaign showed the power of a centrally managed campaign that could respond to local tastes and engage with consumers. It demonstrates how superior marketing can drive sales and deliver a striking return on investment.

What's more, Hiroshi Okuda's corporate goal edges ever closer: Toyota is predicted to eclipse General Motors as the world's number one car-maker, with US sales alone expected to have risen by between 5 and 10 per cent in 2006.

P&G: A SOAP OPERA WITH A HAPPY ENDING

Background

At the dawn of the new millennium, P&G stock was falling dramatically. The company had lost its way at the end of the 1990s following a programme of 'innovation, stretch and change' that had resulted in P&G losing 50 per cent of its value – a staggering $70 billion.

P&G had lost sight of the basics under its ambitious 'Organization 2005' programme, so it had taken its focus off the very brands that had helped it to rise to prominence in the first place. Instead, it was investing its resources into peripheral activities. It was making money from its best-established brands and spending it on other new business efforts.

Challenge

In 2000, two consecutive profit warnings gave P&G the wake-up call it needed.

It finally realized that its business model was not able to sustain high levels of top-line growth. New technologies were putting pressure on its innovation budgets. Its R&D productivity had levelled off, and its innovation success rate – the percentage of new products that had met financial objectives – had stagnated at about 35 per cent. Squeezed by nimble competitors, flattening sales, lacklustre new launches and a quarterly earning miss, it had lost more than half of its market capitalization when its stock slid from $118 to $52 a share.

Solution

Part one: sharpening the corporate focus: staying where the growth is

AG Lafley, P&G's chief executive who succeeded Durk Jager in 2000, spearheaded a new agenda in 2001 that focused on core business, leading brands, biggest markets and top retailers.

Lafley explains:

> The first choice we made was that we're going to grow from our core. We'd been taking cash out of our core businesses and reinvesting it in new business, chasing higher levels of growth. I said 'No, we generally do better in businesses we know the best.' The core businesses at that time were fabric care, feminine care, haircare and baby care.

The team decided to concentrate on building the core brands to be worth at least $1 billion in sales per annum. In 2000, P&G had 10 brands that represented half of its sales and more than half of its profits.

P&G sells in 160 countries, making it difficult to figure out where it should concentrate. The new management team, under Lafley's leadership, recognized that 16 countries account for 80 per cent of its sales, so the company decided to concentrate on its core brands in those markets.

Part two: broadening into beauty

P&G's roots are firmly entrenched in detergent brands such as Tide. As part of its new strategy, it diverted its attention into the fast-growing, higher-margin beauty, health care and personal care sectors.

Part three: attracting lower-income consumers

P&G wanted to drive demand for its products in emerging markets such as Brazil, Russia, India, China and Mexico. Product innovation and branding would underpin its strategies in these markets. Other crucial decisions emphasized an open innovation model in which the company would seek 50 per cent of its new ideas from outside the company and accentuate its leadership development activities.

Jim Stengel, P&G's Global Marketing Officer, told analysts at a Q1 2003 meeting attended by his chief executive and his chief financial officer that every marketing spend at P&G was assessed for its ROI. Transparency rose up the corporate agenda in every department; the marketing teams were no exception.

Results

Five years after its profit warnings, P&G's results showed across-the-board market share growth. Indeed, while its closest rival, Unilever, was suffering from a 36 per cent sales slump after the 'path to growth' strategy had floundered, P&G was busy broadening its product port-folio by snapping up Gillette, a purchase that made it the world's biggest toiletries and cosmetics brand. The acquisition gave P&G a 13 per cent market share.

Revenue was up by 40 per cent; it had doubled its annualized profits and created $60 billion of shareholder value and $30 billion cash flow.

And the future looks sustainable. In 2000, it had just 10 billion-dollar brands. Prior to its purchase of Gillette in 2005, this number had risen to 17.

Its beauty care and health care category sales doubled, increasing from just over a third (36 per cent) in 1998 to be responsible for over half (51 per cent) of P&G's total sales.

New product and marketing innovation in leading brands

P&G's Tide brand had been the number one laundry brand in the United States for over 50 years. In 2003, P&G built Gain to be the United States' second-favourite laundry brand. Gain continues to grow.

Febreze and Swiffer were P&G's big launches in the home care brands category and they have become market leaders. Febreze innovated in air care, while Swiffer has extended its product range into dusters and Swiffer Sweep and Vac.

Developing markets

P&G has become the biggest consumer packaged goods company in 17 developing markets, including Russia, China and Mexico. Volume in China and Russia has more than doubled in the past three years.

Beauty, health care and personal care

P&G's leadership in health care is being strengthened. Despite aggressive competitive activity, US market share of heartburn relief brand Priolsec OTC continues to grow. The osteoporosis medicine Actone now has a global share of almost 30 per cent.

Beauty care is a fast-growing business within P&G. P&G Beauty grew from being worth $10 billion in 2001 to $17 billion in 2004.

Olay deserves special mention. P&G has sold more Olay products in the last five years than in the brand's 50-year life before that, by moving into the prestige skin care market – a sector that accounts for more than 40 per cent of the global skin care market and is heavily populated by premium products at matching prices. The Total Effects range was born and promised to 'fight the 7 signs of ageing'.

In his book *Lovemarks: The future beyond brands*, Kevin Roberts, the Worldwide CEO of Saatchi & Saatchi, comments: 'The Total Effects launch was a phenomenal success, proving the ability of Olay to attract the elusive prestige consumer. Sales were 53 per cent higher in sophisticated prestige markets such as New York, Los Angeles and Chicago' (2004: 188).

This transformation, spearheaded by organizational change and enhanced strategic thinking on how best to approach its global marketing, helped P&G to become a player again.

O2: HOW A £17.7 BILLION BRAND WAS BORN

Background

Far-fetched as it may sound, O2 is the story of how a £4 billion brand transformed into a £17.7 billion brand in the space of just four years. Maunder *et al* reveal how the foundations for this growth were established in their Grand Prix-winning 2004 IPA Effectiveness Paper *O2: It only works if it all works – how troubled BT Cellnet transformed into thriving O2*.

Challenge

In 2001, mmO2 plc – the new name for BT Wireless – was demerged from British Telecom. The following April, the new brand launched as O2. When BT demerged the business, it had a poor reputation. It struggled on all the key metrics: new connections, total subscriber base, non-voice transactions, average revenue per user, and revenue.

O2 needed to relaunch itself as an attractive brand that would play a key role in reversing the fortunes of the beleaguered mobile network.

It was looking to custom-build and fully integrate its brand. Through its visual integration – an approach that is summed up in the internal mantra 'It only works if it all works' – it planned to build rapid awareness. Product investment needed to provide attractive products and tariffs, as well as build a long-term brand.

Solution

O2 set out to become the most 'enabling' brand in the marketplace, facilitating the customer's communication, work and leisure time. This set it apart from other mobile networks that were plugging their mobile vision, technical innovation and product offers such as airtime and new tariffs in ongoing attempts to attract short-term sales.

Susie Moore, UK Head of Brand and Marketing Communications at O2, comments:

> Customers were fed up with promises; they just wanted an enabling brand so they could do what they wanted. In 2002, there were lots of telecoms brands promising things. There was a quote in a piece of

customer research that we did where a customer said: 'My phone is as essential to me as my house keys and wallet; I wouldn't leave home without it.' Phones are now essential for life, and our philosophy has primarily been about putting the customer at the heart of everything.

Internally, O2 adopted the four I's to help it achieve this goal:

- Insight-led marketing promotions that made it easier for the consumer to understand, such as Happy Hour, which promoted free texts between 7 pm and 8 pm for new joiners, and Pay & Go Wild, which offered free calls and texts for £10 a month paid by direct debit. Bolt Ons were another innovation to be born out of Insight and were designed to reward long-term customers with discounts. Bolt Ons allowed regular texters to gain discounts of up to 60 per cent by buying bundles of text messages in advance. When picture messaging took off, O2 encouraged people to see the technology as simply another means of human expression and invited them to 'invent their own language'. These communication approaches were a huge departure from what BT Cellnet had historically done: manufacturer-led, conventional approaches that opted to lead with a technological capability rather than a customer benefit.
- Iconic imagery. The distinctive blue bubbles appeared on every piece of O2 communication, giving it instant stand-out in a crowded sector.
- Individual. All advertising ran the same promotion, so communication didn't compete. Mobile networks had traditionally suffered pile-ups of tactical offers targeting different segments of their customer base. O2's new image was dedicated to keeping communication simple and straightforward.
- Integrated. O2 sought consistency across all channels, including advertising, in-store and sponsorship.

Susie Moore adds: 'We wanted to present an imagery that was like a breath of fresh air, something which went against all of the negatives associated with mobiles and technology. We wanted to show we were doing it in a fresh and different way.'

Results

The O2 share price outperformed the FTSE 100, Vodafone, Orange and BT. Even the competition noticed the contribution made by the brand.

Hans Snook, the founder of Orange, complimented O2 on the 'superb job' that it had done.

Despite O2's share of voice being just 14 per cent, Millward Brown calculated that, based on its advertising impact, O2's effective share of voice was 33 per cent. Because O2 had established itself so rapidly in the market, it could spend less than its competitors and yet still be firmly centre stage.

An Accenture MROI Group study in 2002 that reviewed the effectiveness of telecoms' marketing commented: 'The O2 launch has been the most successful mobile brand launch that Accenture's ROI group has seen. Based on numerous studies that we have conducted, the brand is rare in exceeding our most optimistic targets. The results are testament to the potency of the brand identity and advertising creative.'

The Accenture study also indicated that, if O2 had run advertising of a similar nature to BT Cellnet, it would have needed to spend three times as much to achieve similar levels of awareness, and it would have taken four times as long.

And this is the tip of the iceberg. The lifetime value of O2 customers is expected to continue and to underpin revenue and margin for years to come. A Holmes & Cook report estimated that O2's investment in communications will generate at least £4.8 billion incremental margin over the long term. The ultimate payback is expected to be 62:1.

Not only was O2's relaunch successful in driving short-term sales, but it also secured long-term, brand-led growth. In February 2003, *The Times* commented: 'Already O2 is unimaginable from the scrappy wireless division that was de-merged from BT one year ago.' In May 2004, the *Financial Times* added: 'Not long ago, mmO2 was the ugly step-sister of Europe's mobile operators... Now it's increasingly looking like Cinderella... despite increasing competition from the likes of 3, the company recorded a 16 per cent increase in revenues to £3.2 billion on the back of a 10 per cent increase in new customers.'

Yet the most substantial return so far came when O2 was sold to Telefonica, a deal that was rubber-stamped in March 2006. Telefonica, the Spanish telecom with interests mainly in southern Europe and Latin America, paid £17.7 billion for O2. At the time, this was Europe's largest all-cash takeover.

'Intangible assets' – including the brand, staff and management – were said to be worth £8 billion of this momentous price tag. Considering O2's brand equity, Telefonica now plans to leverage the equity that O2 has built up by rebranding Telefonica's non-Spanish-speaking business to O2.

O2 shows how strong marketing can not only deliver a positive return on investment in terms of the metrics of a business, but also boost staff morale, the esteem of the public, an ability to sustain competitive advantage and the potential to deliver future earnings.

BRITISH AIRWAYS: DEALING WITH TURBULENCE

Background

British Airways often finds itself confronted by extraordinary challenges that place huge demands on its marketing team. In the first few years of the new millennium, many events had conspired to hit the company hard. Global recession, SARS, 9/11, the war in Iraq and the explosion of low-cost, no-frills airlines had all played a part in denting the business performance of British Airways.

Woody Harford, BA's Senior Vice President Commercial in North America, remembers the immediate aftermath of 9/11: 'We were fighting for our existence. Customers had stopped travelling and the revenue fell through the floor. We had enormous debt from buying new aircraft in the mid-90s and things were precarious. We faced a real challenge with how to rebuild the business.'

As Day, Storey and Edwards (2004) explain, in 2002 BA declared a loss on European services of £244 million. The airline dropped out of the FTSE 100 and some analysts thought its days were numbered, particularly in the light of other airlines such as Swissair, KLM and Sabena being sold or merged. If it was to stay in the air, BA had to take drastic action.

Challenge

In the first half of 2002, budget airlines in the UK accounted for 73 per cent of advertising spend, tempting consumers to jump on planes for short-haul breaks at negligible cost. The economy sector showed phenomenal growth, while BA was beginning to look increasingly old-fashioned with its 'frills' and higher-cost flights.

BA's Future Size & Shape initiative restructured its business operations. This included 13,000 job cuts and adjustments to its routes in an attempt to slash costs by £650 million.

The airline didn't advertise at all between September 2001 and January 2002 and, like other transatlantic airlines, had been hard hit by fears and rumours about further terrorist attacks. In the United States, it introduced 'fly when you're ready', which allowed customers greater flexibility about when they travelled as a direct response to the terrorist threat.

In the UK, BA had to make a decision about whether or not to compete with the likes of Ryanair and easyJet by offering short-haul flights within Europe.

Research showed that, while price was important to consumers, so were other factors such as centrally located airports, allocated seating and punctuality. Passengers also liked being offered in-flight food and goodie bags for kids, and BA was trusted to deliver on these counts. Harford notes: 'We want to deliver products and services that enhance the experience of travelling. We're not – and are never going to be – a low-cost carrier like easyJet or Ryanair, but we do offer significant value.'

Solution

BA altered its business model to appeal to the budget airline customer while not veering too far from its brand proposition and actually *becoming* a budget airline. Advertising started to drive sales online rather than to travel agents, minimizing third-party costs. And, to push volume, the new revenue model pivoted on the cheapest sales on any given flight being sold as early as possible.

'Frills' were repositioned as 'service that matters', and BA's low prices were a constant source of surprise in the advertising. In TV work, the gravelly-toned US writer and satirist PJ O'Rourke commented on consumers' frustrations with low-cost airlines, while poster work advertised the competitive flight prices in large print. More non-traditional media were employed, such as ATMs, the BA Destinations Report – a branded content production on Sky News – and the travel page in *Time Out*. BA's TV ads also topped and tailed ad breaks to maximize impact. In total, 10 touchpoints were used; historically BA would have used three.

Results

The campaign at first halted and then reversed BA's sales decline. Consumers correctly identified the ads and flight prices in qualitative research, and opinions of BA improved. BA started to fight back against the no-frills operators, while also managing to stay relevant to business flyers and long-haul customers.

Online booking took off around the new campaign, with more consumers booking flights directly at ba.com, which now offered an improved fare-booking engine.

Econometric analysis allowed the power of the TV work to be quantified. If BA had not advertised, it would have lost over £11.7 million in sales.

Advertised routes versus non-advertised routes were also compared, and passenger data were analysed to see whether routes had received advertising and, if so, through which media. The data indicated that the combination of TV, press and radio was the most effective media mix for BA's message, and that all media mixes outperformed the non-advertised routes.

The value reappraisal campaign also accounted for a greater uplift in bookings than the effect of the price reductions, so informing consumers about the low prices generated more sales than actually lowering the prices.

The campaign not only revitalized BA's commercial performance, but it also influenced the competition, most notably the budget airlines, which issued new price initiatives that eroded their profit margins in autumn 2002. The media took a less harsh line when they reported on BA, and the carrier was named 'best low-cost airline' in a reader poll in the *Guardian* and the *Observer*. Internally, employees were motivated when BA showed it could kick against the competition.

Before the value reappraisal campaign in 2002, British Airways had been valued on the stock market at a historical low of £1.07 billion. By 2004, it had grown its shareholder value by over £2 billion and was worth £3.11 billion, indicating that the business strategy of restructuring and remarketing BA as an alternative in the short-haul economy sector had generated significant shareholder value.

The campaign showed that BA knows how to borrow the clothes of its competitors without abandoning its core brand values. An Institute of Practitioners in Advertising paper from 2004, 'Climbing above the turbulence', concludes:

> BA has proved the positive contribution that a coherent, aggressive communications campaign can make to the sort of competitive struggle it had on its hands in the short-haul sector. It has learnt that promotion can drive volume, and it has seen the power of a multimedia approach... BA's value reappraisal campaign is a dramatic example of the almost instant

business effectiveness that a well-engineered communications programme can have. When times are very tough, the temptation to withdraw from advertising investment is strong. BA's experience, however, will serve to remind us all of the potential of the communications tools at our disposal.

Since 2004, British Airways has continued to innovate in its communications to drive traffic at the back end of the plane: its passenger numbers – or 'load factor' – for the second quarter of 2006 hit an all-time record, 78.3 per cent.

In the same set of results, BA declared a pre-tax profit of £195 million, a year-on-year increase of 57 per cent. Increased passenger numbers and more demand for business-class travel accounted for the higher profits. The chief executive, Willie Walsh, also singled out the airline's low fares offer in the short-haul market.

BA's ability to take on the low-cost players and yet maintain its appeal as a classy carrier suitable for an upmarket business crowd – particularly through subsequent innovations such as flat beds – has been integral to its return to former glory as one of the world's most profitable airlines. It continues to face its fair share of challenges and criticisms, but, from a business point of view, a consistent marketing message has helped the company to remain in rude health.

IMPOSSIBLE IS NOTHING...

Our four Marketing ROI stars show how marketing works as part of a wider business strategy.

They prove that marketing can give customers, staff and shareholders good reason to stay loyal to companies.

To use the investment analogy introduced in Chapter 2, they prove how marketers can generate profit from loans by using the expertise of their stockbrokers and employing a range of different marketing channels.

They display the characteristics described in the following chapters, which we identify as Marketing ROI best practice. They also practise the eight investor tips outlined in the next chapter.

They offer compelling evidence that marketing can move the needle.

Most importantly of all, they serve as a useful reminder that impossible is nothing.

4

Invest, don't spend:
Applying investment disciplines to marketing budgets

Misguided marketing strategies have destroyed more shareholder value – and probably more careers – than shoddy accounting or shady fiscal practices. In almost every industry – telecommunications, airlines, consumer products, finance – it is easy to point to poor marketing as a major cause of low growth and declining margins.

McGovern *et al*, 2004

In Chapter 2, we made a case for renaming Marketing ROI as 'profit' and treating the marketing budget as a 'loan'. In this chapter, we extend that principle and offer tips about how to apply investment principles to the marketing process. Armed with these, marketers can adopt an investment management approach to their decision making. This will give them a solid foundation to grow into Marketing ROI-fit organizations by showing how marketing can drive shareholder value as opposed to being the *enfant terrible* in the boardroom.

THE ICE CHECKLIST

ICE stands for Identify, Clarify and Establish and is a simple tool to ensure that companies use their product benefits to achieve cut-through. When talk around the boardroom table never veers far from budget cuts, extra cash is not going to be available for marketing. This means that marketers have to become more resourceful to put forward the investment case for marketing.

ICE helps marketers to be clear about the strategy under consideration and their reasons for wanting to invest. For consumers, who get bombarded with over 2,000 ad messages every day, ICE can help to create hooks that may just grab their attention at the right time and place:

- *Identify* points of leverage. Pursue opportunities that could entice and persuade your existing customer base, or build a strategy around a particular product benefit that the competition doesn't have.
- *Clarify* the objectives of the investment. This is a vital exercise. Marketers must ask what the investment is trying to achieve. Who is it targeting? Existing customers or new ones? Is the investment to drive sales or loyalty? How does it fit in with the organization's wider corporate goals?
- *Establish* risk. Calculate the returns from your investment and compare them against not investing, as well as against comparative investments from rivals.

First of all, *identify points of leverage*. Court, Gordon and Perrey in their *McKinsey Quarterly* article 'Boosting returns on marketing investment' (2005) define economic leverage for CEOs as 'allocating capital to the businesses generating highest returns'. In marketing, this means making a serious investment in promoting a product's most buyable characteristics over the competition.

For example, British Airways innovated when it introduced flat beds in business-class cabins and was the first airline to promote this feature. It continues to promote this as a British Airways property and 'owns' it, despite competitive airlines offering similar comfort levels.

Fiji Water, based in Los Angeles and a favourite among Hollywood celebrities, leveraged the purity of the country where it's bottled to drive its purity perception versus the competitors in this crowded sector. Its ads, which run in magazines such as *Esquire*, point out: 'the label says Fiji because it's not bottled in Cleveland'.

In terms of identifying your points of leverage, there are a few vital questions that you need to ask:

- Is there room in the market? If so, where?
- What is truly special, new or different about this product?
- How can you best communicate this product's points of difference?
- Who will be interested in purchasing it?
- If you are appealing to existing customers, how can you use your existing brand equity or heritage to excite their interest?

To perform a successful evaluation, marketers must demonstrate a rounded understanding of their brand drivers. The more compelling the brand drivers – either real or perceived – the better the risk/return equation.

Secondly, *clarify the investment objectives.*

Court, Gordon and Perrey (2005) write: 'Good financial advisers start by asking clients about their investment horizons, growth expectations and appetite for risk. Marketing investments should start with similar questions.'

Asking these questions aligns the goals of marketers with those of the company as a whole. Marketers should be focused on selling marketing's value per se and how it can help deliver a return to their boardrooms.

Setting the investment horizon is almost as important as the growth expectation. The period of payback will dictate the marketing communication choices that are made. Toyota plays a long-term game when setting out its goals. This explains the high degree of consistency in its messaging. Meanwhile, the UK electrical retailer Comet evaluates the success of its advertising on the following week's footfall, demanding immediate and readable results.

Marketing investors can set short- and medium-term metrics that satisfy sales needs and their brand aspirations. O2 looks at both its acquisition results *and* its brand preference scores. It has become highly effective with its marketing communications at both a tactical and a brand level.

Clarifying the investment objectives means determining what outcome you're seeking and making it transparent to colleagues what marketing intends to contribute in terms of profit, how much it's going to cost and how it's going to be measured. Making sure that marketing's investment objectives match corporate goals will integrate marketing more seamlessly with the goals of the rest of the organization. This will help to avoid the silo effect discussed in Chapter 2.

The second part of clarification is distinguishing between growth and maintenance objectives. If you want to grow, your objectives are to increase consumption, increase number of usage occasions and usage per occasion, attract new users and – potentially – launch more products. Maintenance, on the other hand, is about minimum investment levels to keep some share of voice in your sector.

Finally, *establish risk*.

Glossy brochures from financial institutions never fail to warn that 'investments may go down as well as up'. Risk is inherent in all decisions, so for an investor it is impossible to eliminate it entirely. Even the most respected fund managers on Wall Street expect to lose money on some of the stocks that they recommend. No one – marketers included – is immune to risk.

Establishing risk relates back to managing your marketing investments in a similar way to a portfolio of stocks and shares – a concept introduced in Chapter 2.

In marketing, as in investing, there are always several strategies that can be deployed. They will vary using different budget scenarios, different channels or different creative approaches. Some will involve higher or lower perceived risk for the marketing investors. A company's level of comfort with risk will depend on its situation and its CEO. More established brand leaders might feel they are able to afford to take fewer risks but be more consistent in their marketing. In contrast, challenger brands or brands in crisis might need to take bigger risks to have a chance of competing or to execute a turnaround successfully.

An investment adviser explains the '40/40/20' rule as follows: 'Put 40 per cent of your budget in safer bonds and property, 40 per cent in slightly riskier equities and a further 20 per cent in speculative opportunities.'

Marketers can apply this principle to their investments by splitting their budgets 80/20. Eighty per cent can be spent on 'bankers', in other words the marketing channels and media that have proved their effectiveness through measurement that shows they are making a positive return. Among our Marketing ROI stars profiled in Chapter 3, examples that fit in this 80 per cent include Procter & Gamble flagship brands such as Herbal Essences, Tide and Pampers maintaining a presence on TV.

We believe that up to 20 per cent of a marketing budget should be allocated to media and message tests. Court, Gordon and Perrey (2005) write:

> One of the best ways to diagnose a marketing organization's ROI discipline is to assess the extent and quality of the media and messaging tests

in progress at any given time. Some will be simple, such as testing higher levels of expenditure or new media for a proven message, reducing the frequency of mailings to see if the response rates change, and testing a new advertising message in a particular region. Others, such as a simultaneous test of a new message and a new media for a growing segment of profitable customers, are bigger departures from the routine.

Ephron and Pollak in 2003 showed that, for every advertising dollar spent, the returns were just $0.54 in consumer packaged goods and $0.87 for non-consumer packaged goods within a year of the ad appearing. With media planning, copy testing and improved investment choice, that payback could double.

INVESTING IN EXPERIMENTATION

Julian Elliott, the Group Marketing Head of Effectiveness at Lloyds TSB, is a firm believer in investing in experimentation. At Lloyds TSB, there is a leftover 10 per cent of marketing budgets where, as he puts it, 'no one gets fired for spending in the wrong way. It's like a sandpit, a play area where people have got the freedom to experiment with different techniques.'

The amount you decide to invest in experimentation is a movable feast because returns have different investment horizons. For instance, when a TV ad campaign is testing well, any additional activity should help to contribute towards positive returns.

Experimentation can inform future decision making and investment selections. For example, experimenting with a medium that has, to date, never been used by your company but in fact proves to be an effective route to market could dramatically alter investment decisions in subsequent years. It also allows marketers the freedom to keep up with new innovations in marketing and media without fear of being castigated for being profligate.

The return generated by resources that are dedicated to experimentation could in fact be a pleasant surprise for the finance director. Virgin Mobile found this when it created an 'influencer team' of 300 customers to create buzz around its new brand, products and messages. It seeded viral movies online through the www.best-hands.net website, an innovation that attracted more than 4 million customers.

Once you have gone through all the points on your ICE checklist, pay attention to how to measure advertising's payback over the long term.

DECIDE WHETHER YOU NEED TO INVEST IN MARKETING

The time has come for you to present your marketing strategy to the board. You prepare to launch into the case for why the budget should be allocated this way rather than that when your CEO thunders: 'Should we invest in marketing at all?'

Marketing investors will not be thrown by the question because, just as good investors know when to keep their assets in cash and when to invest, good marketers know when marketing is appropriate. Smart marketing investors know when the best course of action is not to market at all and understand that sometimes it's inappropriate to market full stop.

It's the default position of most marketers to think that marketing is always the solution. It's not.

This is not a new theory; it extends back to 1923 – and probably pre-dates that. In *Scientific Advertising*, originally published in 1923, Claude Hopkins (1980) put forward the opinion that advertising was sales-manship, and so it should be measurable. Over 80 years ago, he wrote: 'Force it to justify itself. Compare it with other salesmen. Figure its cost and result. Accept no excuses which good salesmen do not make. Then you will not go far wrong.'

A decision whether to invest or not needs to start with zero-based planning. Before becoming too engrossed in the specifics of a campaign, evaluate what the consequences would be if you did no promotions, and assess the impact on revenues versus other opportunities. Econometric modelling can provide trend analysis that quantifies the full effect of reducing advertising. This should arm you with the information you need to answer the CEO's question confidently.

Dark smoke

Tobacco companies have had to adjust to not being able to advertise their products because regulations have meant that the advertising markets where they traditionally appeared have gone 'dark'. In other words, regulations have been enforced in many territories that have made ads for tobacco products illegal. Some brands responded by advertising as much as possible before the markets went 'dark', and that strategy paid off: the companies found that echoes of their voice remained, even in the darkness. What's more, the advertising restrictions made it almost impossible for new brands to come to market because they couldn't use above-the-line marketing to make themselves visible.

Established tobacco brands that had enjoyed an advertising presence until regulations were enforced weren't losing their market position. In fact they found that it was actually more profitable for them not to advertise.

Food and drink manufacturers in many markets are currently confronting a similar situation. Ads for sugary and fatty products – particularly those that target children – are currently under the spotlight on account of health concerns over obesity. Keeping the volume turned up on their existing marketing activity could stand these products in good stead until any specific advertising legislation is enforced.

MARKETING – AN ALTERNATIVE TO ACQUISITION

Mergers and acquisitions are – rightly or wrongly – regarded as a sure-fire route to value creation. By comparison, there is little evidence that shows how marketing can make companies more valuable entities.

Consultants and venture capitalists size up certain businesses and make decisions about whether they should buy them or not with the funds available to them at a particular time. This decision is based on the principle of whether they could build an equivalent from scratch for a lesser amount of cash. With corporate acquisitions valuing companies on at least two to four times revenues, marketing – if the appropriate investment decisions are made – can easily compete in terms of driving shareholder value.

Look at the success of one of our Marketing ROI stars, O2. In just four years, it quadrupled in value thanks to building up a brand-centric, customer-focused business. Would an acquisition have delivered the same ROI as marketing?

THE LADDER OF INSIGHT

In his 2003 article 'Measuring ROI: where are you on the ladder of insight?', Patrick LaPointe, the editor-in-chief of the journal *MarketingNPV*, writes that there are five levels of ROI measurement:

1. sales tracking, test markets, market research;
2. ad hoc programme and initiative ROI;
3. optimizing resource allocation;
4. brand asset valuation;
5. integrated measurement.

LaPointe writes: 'At the top of the ladder, all marketing activities are planned and measured in an integrated framework that incorporates both short- and long-term return.'

Yet very few companies have made it past level three to evaluate the relative ROI performance of different marketing elements.

Progress is under way. Marketing-mix modelling and optimization are becoming more widespread on both the agency and the client side. Mullen, an Interpublic-owned agency in Massachusetts, has developed a tool that can predict the individual and combined impact of traditional and non-traditional media-mix alternatives. This is no doubt music to the ears of Jim Stengel, P&G's Global Marketing Officer, who bemoans that 'the marketing-mix analysis still primarily looks at how each part of the mix works independently rather than at optimizing how all parts work best together'.

Our observations of successful marketers that have delivered effective ROI have incorporated a number of characteristics that have helped them drive business results and helped them to scale the ladder of insight. These are summarized below and form the backbone of the rest of this book.

OUR EIGHT INVESTOR TIPS TO PROFITABLE MARKETING COMMUNICATIONS

1. Concentrate on *outcomes*, not outputs.
2. Forget consumers, *target customers*.
3. Manage your communication investment *portfolio*.
4. *Differentiate* any way you can.

5. *Engagement* and *experience* are the new 30-second ads.
6. Apply a *'focus investing'* approach.
7. Establish a *measurement* culture.
8. Leverage your *employee* capital.

1. Concentrate on outcomes, not outputs

Brand awareness, ad awareness, coverage and frequency, cost per thousand (or ratings) and cost per click are marketing measures that are often used to justify marketing spend. But these units of measurement are just not as relevant to boards, which are far more interested in one measurement unit: shareholder value.

Refer back to 'ICE' at the beginning of this chapter, specifically the critical step of 'clarifying investment objectives'. Marketers need to have a clear idea of what they want to achieve from their investment right from the start. That can only happen if they have clear measurable objectives that have a direct line of sight to improving profitability.

Many marketers come unstuck at this stage with the unfortunate consequence that their marketing activity becomes more geared towards outputs as opposed to outcomes. In Chapter 5, we argue the case for articulating a business strategy with specific outcomes that build a solid platform for profitable marketing communications.

The non-marketing management of companies must be able to understand and own any metrics adopted. So once marketers start speaking in language that resonates with the rest of the board, the information that they share instantly becomes more meaningful.

2. Forget consumers, target customers

Smart investing is about putting your money into higher-profit, lower-risk opportunities. The best opportunities for growth and profit are your existing customers.

Many companies are preoccupied with acquiring new customers when in fact their resources would be much better deployed if they concentrated on their existing customer base. These customers have already been persuaded to choose your company over the competition, so it follows that they are more inclined to spend money with you.

A strategy that gets closer to 'customers' as opposed to talking to 'consumers' focuses the organization on the front line. Building up customer satisfaction and loyalty can result in extending the lifetime value of a customer. For example, if a customer buys a Toyota in his or her 30s and has a good experience, that customer is more likely to stick with it throughout his or her 40s and 50s. And, if the customer has a *really* good customer experience, he or she will tell friends and family, resulting in more acquisitions.

Marketing to existing customers can fulfil an acquisition function too, whereas marketing with a view only to acquire has no appeal to customers who are already converts. In fact, focusing too much on acquisition can make existing customers feel undervalued: think of a health club that focuses entirely on acquisition. Once new members are paying a monthly fee, some health clubs think there's very little reason to communicate with them other than to try to persuade them to recommend more people to join up. A Mintel report (2006b) on health and fitness clubs in the United States indicates that US health clubs are not meeting the needs of their members and that revenue growth pivots on signing up new customers. This has resulted in revenues per member declining by 10 per cent in the five-year period from 2000 to 2005. Translate that into marketing terms and it's clear to see that looking after existing customers offers more potential for profit.

We develop this idea in Chapter 6.

3. Manage your communication investment portfolio

Marketers have a wide choice of investment options open to them: advertising, direct response, events, sponsorships, PR and digital media, to name but a few. Smart marketing investors evaluate all the potential vehicles and their potential payback before making a commitment to particular investment choices.

Marketing investors also need to be flexible enough to change a particular channel if it isn't working hard enough. If they can see better potential returns in an alternative channel, the investor should be prepared to switch investments to maximize the overall performance of their marketing communication investment portfolio.

There is a growing emphasis on integrated communications in modern marketing practice. The advantage of investing in more integrated communications is that consumers are receiving a consistent brand message across several platforms. The different channels can work collaboratively to maximize marketing's performance.

Evaluating and allocating budgets across a range of different channels require skill and discipline. Tracking each investment through robust measurement tools verifies whether a channel's performance is strong enough to stay within the portfolio.

Stock market investors would not tolerate poorly performing stock from one company, even if their other investments were working hard. Similarly, with a communication portfolio, marketers have to be flexible, and act promptly if one of their investments is underperforming.

Chapter 7 discusses how to approach evaluating and allocating budgets across the different channels.

4. Differentiate any way you can

In his book *The Paradox of Choice: Why more is less* (2004), Barry Schwartz visits his local supermarket and counts 275 varieties of cereal, 175 salad dressings and 175 types of tea bag. The proliferation of consumer choice means that products and services need to get noticed to survive, and marketing plays a critical role here.

The safest investment decisions *appear* to be to follow the crowd. Despite the returns from this strategy being – at best – incremental, this is the course of action chosen by most marketers.

Yet the most impressive profits have been generated by those marketing communications that have eschewed 'safe' marketing choices. As John Hegarty, the Worldwide Creative Director at Bartle Bogle Hegarty suggests, 'When the rest of the world is zigging, you should zag.'

Unfortunately, brands that zag are very much in the minority. Particularly in larger organizations where there is more overlap between products, it becomes much harder to achieve differentiation. The worst-case scenario is when a company's brands end up competing with each other.

As Tim Ambler writes in *Marketing and the Bottom Line* (2004), 'Differentiation lies at the heart of marketing and the consequence is that great marketers are constantly trying new things. Those that work they continue, those that do not, they avoid. Poor marketing does what others do, too little and too late.' He continues: 'Differentiation may not matter to a new brand but a mature brand with a host of imitators needs to keep fresh and separate.'

Don't fall into the trap of safe, expected marketing choices. You're only adding to the commoditization of your product or service. If consumers can't perceive any difference between your brand and a competitor's, then there can't be any advantage. If there's no obvious advantage, your pricing will be pushed downwards.

We provide fresh evidence of how differentiation works to drive Marketing ROI in Chapter 8.

5. Engagement and experience are the new 30-second ads

Capital gains come from creating connections with consumers. Greater accountability can be achieved by focusing less on delivering advertising to audiences and focusing more on *how* consumers receive those messages. That means understanding and utilizing all available consumer touchpoints, from in-store to the internet, mobile phones to magazines.

Consumers' ability to block out advertising has reached Olympian standards, whether it's flicking past ads in the newspaper or zapping through commercial breaks on TV. Consumers have had decades of advertisers trying to sell them things through mass media. Now advertisers have to entice them with a much more powerful proposition.

Engagement and experience are becoming much more potent factors for marketers seeking out consumers. This could translate as a beer brand shunning traditional media in favour of sponsoring a music festival or a sporting event, or Orange Wednesdays that offer brand loyalists two-for-one cinema tickets. Such 3D connections generate value for both customers and companies.

Chapter 9 explores engagement and experience strategies from our Marketing ROI stars, as well as from Starbucks, Nike, Axe (Lynx) and Hewlett-Packard.

6. Apply a 'focus investing' approach

Focus investing is about resisting the temptation to diversify and instead simplifying your marketing portfolio with a collection of proven investments.

We use an analogy from the investment world: Warren Buffett, one of the world's most successful fund managers. He took control of the investment company Berkshire Hathaway 40 years ago. Since then, he has delivered a compound annual return of 24 per cent and is the world's second-richest man with a $41 million fortune. Buffett attributes his success to a focus investing strategy. Having chosen a handful of outstanding stocks, he placed the biggest bets on what he terms his 'highest probability' events.

Buffett is living proof that focusing on one or two things and executing them well generates results. In Chapter 10, we argue that marketers could benefit from this investment approach because realism dictates that there simply aren't enough marketing dollars to support every product and reach every target.

Hans Straberg, the CEO of Electrolux, understood this principle when he was quoted in an article called 'Brand challenge' in *The Economist* on 6 April 2002: 'Our aim is to become a reliable and trusted partner with our customers and retailers. That means we need a few strong brands. We can't support too many.'

Mobile phone handset brands have grasped this principle. Although they may have an extensive range of handsets, the likes of Nokia and Motorola will tend to put the most marketing spend behind the handset with the most innovative design. This is not only to push that particular product; it also does a 'halo' job and promotes the entire portfolio of handsets.

Mobile phone operators also understand that the appeal of a blanket targeting approach is limited in markets that have near-universal penetration. For this reason, Virgin Mobile decided to home in on 16- to 24-year-olds in its marketing rather than to cast its net wide.

In Chapter 10, we provide more detail about how focus investing works from a Marketing ROI perspective.

7. Establish a measurement culture

Different marketing investments need to be evaluated in terms of how they are working now as well as how they are performing against expectations. This will lead to a decision as to whether to maintain or ditch particular elements of the marketing investment portfolio.

Brand-by-brand econometric analysis can play a role here in helping to inform future spend. It can also assist decisions such as determining the advertising versus promotions spend ratio. As Ingrid Murray, the Managing Director at Ninah Consulting, says: 'Modelling is there to help marketers make better – and more creative – decisions.'

There is a fear, she says, of numbers, and this needs to be addressed:

> A lot of people don't want to be told 'what you've been doing historically is not the right thing'. But in fact it's about where they go from here, and what they should do differently in future. The better armed they are to know that, the better chance they have of getting their brand to perform to – or exceed – targets.

Of course, analysis shouldn't be confined to your own brand portfolio. Keeping tabs on the marketplace and a careful watch on what the competition is up to is just as important.

Sales response curves can be built from information such as competitive activity, on-trade and off-trade promotions, and research that indicates whether consumers would feel more inclined to use more of your product on specific occasions. In consumer goods advertising, this method can be an effective way of assessing different strategies over three or five years in terms of deciding whether or not they should invest consistently.

Econometrics and the impact of marketing on cash flow are all useful metrics to the ROI-conscious marketer and will offer insight into what works and what doesn't.

In Chapter 11, we suggest how to hard-wire the most useful metrics into your overall marketing programme.

8. Leverage your employee capital

If a marketing strategy motivates staff, customers have a better experience and are more inclined to be loyal. If customers are more loyal, they generate more profit for the company. If more profit is generated for the company, shareholder value increases.

Retail outlets and customer-facing businesses in particular have to rely heavily on creating a consumer pull.

In Chapter 12, we argue that employees should be regarded as part of the target market for big advertising campaigns. We cite four examples of companies that have driven value by appealing internally as well as externally – Schering-Plough, Tesco, BUPA and Halifax – and also talk about how our Marketing ROI stars have employed this tactic.

USE THESE TOOLS...

For marketers, ICE and these eight investor tips provide an easily achievable framework for adopting an investment approach to marketing communications.

Combined, they facilitate decision making, strategy direction and the alignment of marketing goals with wider corporate objectives. Implementing these straightforward tools will give greater credence to the case for marketing, and help to lift the fog that has shrouded Marketing ROI for as long as advertising has existed.

5

Concentrate on outcomes, not outputs

An agency colleague shared with us a story about meeting with the KFC franchise marketing board – a group that represented the restaurant owners and franchisees. As each restaurant contributed a percentage of sales to fund the advertising, the ad agency and the marketing director regularly met with this group to 'sell in' the advertising.

These meetings were often tense events for both the agency and the marketing director. Both parties were responsible for developing the marketing communication plans and advertising work. Hard-nosed store managers and retailers had little time for advertising executives from London, so when they met their worlds collided.

When presenting the media plans, the agency executive defended his choice of TV schedules. He insisted that they would deliver the optimum level of coverage and frequency against the core target demographic while delivering a low cost per thousand. According to the agency's modelling of past advertising, this strategy would deliver the targeted awareness levels for the campaign.

One of the franchisees interrupted him to ask: 'Can you buy a spot in the middle of *Who Wants to Be a Millionaire?*'

Our agency colleague responded: 'I'm not sure if that particular programme stacks up on our modelling system.'

The franchisee pointed out: 'All I know is that whenever we put a spot in that programme more people come into the store. I sell more chicken and we make more money.'

The moral of the story? An over-reliance on soft metrics can obstruct the ultimate corporate goal of driving sales and profit. Some marketers find themselves focusing far too much on outputs as surrogates for marketing payback at the expense of keeping tabs on what's driving growth and profit.

With the drive towards greater accountability, some organizations are trapped into an over-obsession with metrics; everyone so desperately wants to prove that everything works that they lose sight of their actual goal and end up targeting and measuring the wrong things.

This obsession gets in the way of companies realizing Marketing ROI, or profit.

The theme of this chapter is about not losing sight of that end-goal by learning to focus on outcomes rather than outputs.

OUTPUT OBSESSIONS

The world is divided between people who see marketing as a cost and people who see it as an investment. Every marketer in the world will say that their budget isn't big enough, but they have got to know how much to spend; they can't just spend money and not know what's most effective. That's input/output marketing when all that really matters is the outcome.
Rob Rees, Troubleshooter, Interim Marketing/Commercial Director and Co-Founder, Freestyle Marketing

One of the key foundations of Marketing ROI is putting in place a structure with the right measures based on outcomes rather than outputs. In our view, awareness, coverage, cost per response and brand equity are outputs; they are not outcomes that marketing should target. They don't sustain financial scrutiny and they aren't tied into delivering the ROI – or profit – expected from marketing investments.

Boards want to understand how marketing is directly increasing sales, improving profitability and enhancing shareholder value. Marketers trying to justify their investments using these metrics will find themselves confronted by the CFO and the very real prospect of having their budgets slashed when they fail to prove a link between the required input (investment) and the desired outcome (profit).

OUTPUTS THAT DRIVE THE WRONG MARKETING

Being overly focused on outputs can drive the wrong sort of marketing investment decisions.

A particular objective can launch a marketer down a particularly narrow path before he or she has had a proper chance to assess all the possible options. Many years ago, when a colleague was planning for a nappies brand, the client set an objective of maximizing awareness. The solution was always going to be television with a solid mix of prime time because there was no other medium that could match TV's efficiency in terms of driving awareness against the broad target audience.

To engage with new parents or parents-to-be, particularly mothers, ads in baby magazines and on outdoor sites near maternity hospitals were a no-brainer. Somewhat surprisingly, they proved to be a remarkably difficult sell.

But consider what proportion of the marketing budget was wasted in reaching people on prime-time television who may well have been in the right demographic (16- to 34-year-old women) but who were definitely not in the market to buy. This is a textbook example of how an output can steer a particular course of action at the expense of achieving the best outcome.

Outputs are often used as the endgame rather than as various checkpoints on the path to profit. This is where we question brand building. Too often it is used as an excuse to duck the issue of driving ROI. We're told that advertising the brand will create equity with the consumer, which will *eventually* lead to sales and long-term brand strength. Yet all too often, these assumptions are made with little or no evidence of a direct line of sight. As a Coca-Cola executive once said in one of our meetings: 'That's nice, but we don't live in the land of eventually.'

Devastatingly, because marketing professionals tend to over-rely on these 'outputs', boards take them less seriously, meaning that it becomes much harder for them to get their budgets approved. All in all, being focused on outputs can turn into a vicious circle where marketers talk only about the brand. Consequently, their results-focused colleagues stop listening to them, preferring to remain cynical about how marketing can improve business performance.

Marketers have responded by leaping on to the ROI bandwagon. In reality, this has been more superficial than beneficial. *Defining ROI*, a survey of US marketers conducted by Forrester Research and the Association of National Advertisers, showed that, when it came to defining what was meant by ROI, 66 per cent said it related to incremental sales. Fifty-seven per cent, however, defined ROI as changes in brand awareness, 40 per cent said it related to lead generation and 30 per cent of the marketers considered coverage and frequency of their advertising schedules were what they meant by ROI. Sales, effectiveness, response and efficiency risk become interchangeable terms with ROI when marketers attempt to justify their spending decisions. This only does the marketing profession more harm than good when they're presenting to their boardroom colleagues.

Metrics such as these simply don't hold up against other parts of the company, particularly where the likes of Six Sigma disciplines are being applied. Unhelpful metrics are often used because they are easier to measure or because sales are affected by other non-marketing factors such as distribution and pricing that will influence sales beyond marketing communications. Or perhaps marketers feel more comfortable targeting outputs rather than committing to harder measures of success.

WHAT'S THE DIFFERENCE BETWEEN AN OUTCOME AND AN OUTPUT?

Marketing and the Bottom Line (Ambler, 2004) points out that there is often a contradiction between what is measured and what it is considered important to measure. He points to the example of NHS waiting lists in the UK: targets were met but actual waiting times increased and non-urgent patients were prioritized over more urgent cases.

Think back to the KFC marketer. An outcome of the fast food restaurants advertising in *Millionaire* was that it sold more chicken. An output was the media agency's carefully selected media plan based on coverage and frequency. Being too output-driven hinders marketers from developing an instinct for the right course of action that could lead to a better outcome, in other words increased profits.

CREATING A MARKETING ROI CULTURE

ROI-conscious marketing investors can balance the holy trinity of understanding how, when and where to use metrics, applying creative and inspirational thinking and sound commercial decision making. They understand that well-executed marketing enables and empowers a business, an understanding that validates investing in a process that proves that marketing delivers value.

Yet just as with alcoholics attending their first Alcoholics Anonymous meeting, the first step is acknowledging that there's a problem. Despite Herculean efforts and some commendable progress, Marketing ROI remains something that just isn't being delivered. According to Rob Rees: 'Most marketers aren't serious at all about ROI. They get their budget approved and then they just go and spend it.'

For an ROI culture to be created, marketers must work to make marketing outcomes more transparent, more commercial and more aligned to the business strategies. This entails a bigger step than changing what's in place already; in most companies, it will mean starting completely from scratch.

SETTING THE RIGHT METRICS

Brand awareness, brand equity, cost per acquisition and market share are common metrics used by marketers, which offer certain insights into brand performance, but which are limited in how they relate to *business* performance. Below, we assess the benefits and the drawbacks of each one.

The illusion of awareness

Having worked with huge global brands such as Coca-Cola, McDonald's, Sony and Nokia, we find that they spend very little time thinking about brand awareness. These brands have phenomenal ubiquity and, as a result, they are less interested in consumers being able to recall their brands. They spend more of their time wanting to understand the sales pull-through of their marketing communication.

According to a *Journal of Advertising Research* validation study of 1,165 aired TV commercials in 16 different product categories, published in MSW Research's newsletter *Topline* in 2005, brand recall's contribution to brand sales is, on average, 25 per cent, while persuasion's is 75 per cent. Persuasion is clearly a much more important metric than recall because it is the essence of the brand's unique positioning and user benefit. Persuasion also reflects how convincingly advertising delivers the strategic drivers to the consumer. Yet recall has the advantage of being easier to measure.

Dotcom advertising on the eve of the new millennium emphasized just how overrated brand awareness could be. The new brands paid a fortune to advertise in the 1999 Super Bowl, which contributed to pushing up their share price temporarily. That year's game was dominated by dotcom brands, all of which had pretty much disappeared a few years later.

That's not to say that brand awareness has no value; it's relevant when launching a new brand, particularly if there is a genuine point of difference or a need to launch quickly. A pharmaceutical brand, for instance, might need to make consumers aware of a new drug that cures a particular ailment.

Brand awareness can also play an important role in highly competitive or cluttered categories where there's little discernible differentiation between brands. For example, in the haircare category there is high switching and low differentiation, so advertising can play a part in driving awareness.

But, in general, there is an over-assumption that awareness *is* the objective because there is often only nominal correlation between brand awareness and ROI.

The recency rationale

It's no coincidence that the original title for John Philip Jones's 1995 book *When Ads Work* was 'The Advertising Trigger'. In the book, Jones revealed his 'recency theory', which homed in on the concept that most advertising works by influencing the brands selected by consumers who have cash in their pocket and are geared up to make a purchase. Consumer packaged sectors are characterized by short sales cycles, tough competition, lower loyalty and lower involvement.

So one of the most effective advertising strategies for established brands with strong familiarity was to place advertising at the point closest to where the shopper could buy. This could be a series of Clinique ads decorating the escalator at a station near a department store, an in-store promotion for a new brand of snack food, or an interstitial ad for car hire on a travel website, which appears when the user has just bought a holiday.

Brand equity: what's it really worth?

Brand equity is often used as a measure for a brand campaign, but in fact it can't be used as a surrogate for sales because it offers no consistent or universal means to measure. For instance, Interbrand's established Brand Valuation Model and the recent addition to the fray, the Millward Brown Optimor (MBO), adopt different formulae when defining 'brand equity'. MBO, in its list of Top 100 Global Brands – compiled from Millward Brown's Brandz database – includes entries that Interbrand has never featured in its ranking, such as Wal-Mart and China Mobile. The lists also differ on the world's biggest brand, with Interbrand citing Coca-Cola and Millward Brown, Microsoft. There are at least half a dozen different formulae for calculating brand equity. If the methodologies can't agree, it's understandable that boards answerable to shareholders can't take brand equity as a serious business metric.

The other factor to consider is that brand equity is boosted by several factors beyond marketing communication: sales staffs, call centres, the CEO's visibility (which is particularly relevant to companies like Virgin, Microsoft and Apple where the CEO is rarely out of the limelight), product performance, word of mouth and other uncontrollable touch-points. As a result, there's no consistent cause-and-effect relationship between improved brand equity and improved profit.

For a CFO who is accustomed to metrics such as internal rate of return (IRR) or economic value added (EVA), brand equity simply can't match up.

The trouble with cost per acquisition

This is a useful metric for gauging the relative efficiency of different marketing channels. However, it's worth being slightly wary of becoming too fixated on acquisition. Not only does this exclude the value offered by existing customers, but it also shifts the focus on to the new customers as opposed to profitability.

For instance, the research company Experian estimates that it costs a credit card company at least £100 to take on a new customer. Bear in mind that this new credit cardholder might be someone who pays off the balance on time and in full every month, and it's clear that he or she represents limited lifetime value to a credit card company. Output-obsessed marketers often find themselves paying to acquire new customers as a means in itself rather than a means to an end. This makes acquisition a costly business with no guaranteed returns.

The mirage of market share

Being market-leading doesn't necessarily mean that a company is the most profitable. For instance, General Motors sells more cars than any other car manufacturer, but its financials have been less than impressive over the last few years. According to the article entitled 'On a collision course' published on economist.com on 4 April 2006, it lost $10.6 billion in 2005.

Targeting market share isn't wrong, but ROI is about growing profit and sometimes that involves rethinking how to do business. There has to be a strategic reason why marketing to maximize market share is commercially the right business decision.

USEFUL METRICS

Sergio Zyman, the consultant and former Coke marketing officer who helped to boost Coke's worldwide annual sales volume from 9 billion to 15 billion cases, famously defined marketing success as 'selling more stuff to more people more often for more money more efficiently'.

The metrics that demonstrate levers that closely match these objectives are:

- intention to buy;
- brand penetration (or trial);
- repeat volume;
- loyalty;
- retention rate;
- price premium (relative price);
- customer profitability.

Each of these metrics can be tied to increased purchase, revenue or profitability. They also provide a basis to measure marketing communication performance and ability to target the communication at a specific objective.

In Simon London's article 'Enterprise drives home the service ethic' published in the *Financial Times* on 2 June 2003, Andy Taylor, Chairman and CEO of Enterprise Rent-A-Car, commented: 'In the 1990s, we were a billion dollar company; growing fast, profitability was good. Background noise suggested our customer service had started to slip. The Enterprise Service Quality Index (ESQI) was a breakthrough. Over the years, we have refined it until now we ask customers only two questions: "Are you satisfied with our service? Would you come back?"'

Quantitative data will reflect how a company is performing now, but it's the *qualitative* analysis that will hint at future business performance.

TURNING METRICS INTO OBJECTIVES

Marketers can always find a good story – even with a poor marketing performance. Explanations typically include: 'the campaign didn't sell, but we got fantastic awareness' or 'the awareness figures were lower than expected, but we got good ratings on likeability of the ads'.

Marketers are often guilty of introducing metrics at the end of a campaign to help retro-fit results. Yet for metrics to work usefully, they need to be in place right at the start of the process (see Chapter 11). They need to reflect the strategic expectations of marketing and have a strong sense of direction. Metrics need to be *proactive* rather than defensive.

Selecting a handful of primary metrics that can be tracked across all marketing efforts can work as a springboard for creating measurable objectives. Metrics need to drive marketing strategies rather than just be a measure for it. The more single-minded the metrics are, the sharper the marketing communication. Keeping all tactics focused on supporting strategies and objectives puts marketing investors in a much stronger position to defend their budget. A marketing plan that incorporates success measurements also allows marketers to review their accomplishments late in the year, rather than being on the defensive come budget allocation time.

TARGETING THE *RIGHT* OUTCOME

When it came to planning its marketing communication campaign, Toyota's upmarket Lexus range focused its communication strategy against a key stage of the customer journey.

Instead of trying to *drive awareness* and compete with the bigger budgets and the more established German luxury car marques, Lexus took a different route. In other words, it didn't opt for the 'traditional' choices of pan-European business press and cable TV channels.

It had unearthed a valuable insight that led to the competitive advantage for this campaign: potential car buyers who went to test-drive a Lexus had a significantly higher conversion rate to purchase than those who test-drove a BMW, Audi or Mercedes. This heavily influenced the communication strategy.

Focusing the communication investment more heavily behind getting the target to test-drive a Lexus not only provided a more direct line of sight to drive vehicle sales versus their competitors but also gave the platform far more focused and differentiated marketing. The sales results that followed were exceptional.

Case study: Lexus Europe – Driving sales, not awareness

Challenge

Lexus regards its competitive set as the larger-selling and more established European car marques of Audi, Mercedes and BMW. Yet it outperforms all three on its sales conversion to test drives. Lexus faced up to the reality that it was less likely to be placed on a consideration list versus better-established brands. To attract potential customers, it had to focus on the driving experience and the value/luxury equation synonymous with its cars.

Lexus needed to get people closer to its brand to generate test drives, which would then convert into sales across Europe. Instead of waiting for potential customers to find the Lexus, the campaign decided to put its target market in the vehicle. It needed to familiarize the target with the benefits that the Lexus had to offer as a contemporary luxury car.

Solution

This was to surround the target audience with Lexus cars while they were travelling on business and in key holiday destinations. This gave the target constant opportunities to feel the Lexus experience and to gain direct access to the brand via chauffeur-driven cars. To qualify, registration was required, giving Lexus an opportunity for data capture.

As well as creating partnerships with traditional media outlets, ZenithOptimedia, Lexus's media agency, joined forces with six-star hotels, restaurants, ski resorts and airports across the French and Italian Rivieras and the Swiss Alps – the prime holiday spots for the 'upper liberals' – Europe's affluent 35- to 55-year-olds and the core target market.

Magazines and online featured a bespoke booklet that showcased summer activity featuring the SC430 sports coupé and the LS430 limousine on the French and Italian Rivieras, and the RX300 4WD and the SC430 sports coupé, which made their winter debut on the ski slopes. The booklet highlighted the Lexus chauffeur service that featured in the participating hotels and encouraged the more affluent targets to use it. Lexus models were also on display inside airports at those holiday destinations with test drives and chauffeur request cards on display. All activity was measurable from leads generated at airports, individuals who had utilized the chauffeur services at hotels and online requests for more information and test drives.

Results

The results surpassed expectations. Over 5,800 quality leads for test drives were generated, representing over 10 per cent of the annual lead quota. What's more, in keeping with Lexus experience prior to the campaign, leads generated achieved a much higher conversion rate compared with general test drives.

HOW TO FOCUS ON OUTCOME-LED MARKETING

The Lexus example clearly shows that focusing on appropriate outcomes can improve the return on your marketing investment. These seven steps can help you to achieve similar goals by implementing an outcome-led approach:

1. *Build a team.* Unite stakeholders including finance, brand management, market research and C-suite management.

2. *Unify the ROI agenda:*
   - Debate and agree a strategy.
   - Set realistic and quantifiable objectives.
   - Prioritize outcomes.
3. *Establish metrics:*
   - Determine data sources and frequency of collection.
   - Set targets based on established benchmarks and historical performance based on a specific time frame.
   - Align budgets with targets.
4. *Initiate marketing communication development:*
   - Brief agencies.
   - Use insight in a coherent way.
   - Revisit metrics.
5. *Establish the marketing dashboard.* Align the dashboard with the cross-functional team so that it works across different departments.
6. *Deploy data strategically.* Once the campaign has launched, improve and optimize its performance based on data.
7. *Review the process.*

Using these steps gives you flexibility and, because the team is made up from different business functions, it will make it easier to align your marketing with your stakeholders to drive the Marketing ROI. Many of these steps were evident in the hugely successful New Steel campaign that ran in the United States.

Case study: New Steel – Aligning stakeholders behind the marketing investment

In Moore and Allsop's paper 'The ROI imperative: how to build measurable value', presented at the ESOMAR Annual Congress in Lisbon in September 2004, the authors share the example of New Steel, the winner of the 2001 Advertising Research Foundation's David Ogilvy Grand Trophy for 'best demonstration of success in delivering advertising returns'.

A collaborative effort from Wirthlin Worldwide (research and strategy consulting), GSD&M (advertising agency) and Porter Novelli (public relations) was praised for working with a consortium of 70 steel manufacturers in the United States, which had joined forces to drive demand for steel as a raw material.

The example shows how New Steel implemented a process to drive outcome-led marketing by following many of the steps outlined above.

Build a team

Key stakeholders united on the agenda and expectations and communicated regularly. Ten meetings took place with the leaders of the various industry and supplier groups that were funding the programme, alongside four briefing meetings with the CEOs of the different steel companies.

Unify the ROI agenda

The consortium set the objective to make steel the 'material of choice' for the packaging, car manufacture, construction, housing and appliance industries.

An initial investment of $20 million a year defined the terms of success and introduced surrogate measures. The consortium asked itself 'What actions or outcomes will need to occur to make it worth the investment?'

Here, they drew on the experience and expertise of teams that had implemented similar campaigns, and consulted previous case studies. They also set methods and models on which strategy and measurement would be based, and built frequent and direct interaction into the process, with people driving strategy and execution.

Establish metrics, marketing dashboard

A research consultant made recommendations about the methodology. By meeting with key executives, the right expectations were set.

The campaign's goals were articulated in measurable terms so that everyone involved could buy into what the campaign was trying to achieve. The metrics were set based on significant improvement against the current market value and agreed with the stakeholders. They included the following:

● Awareness had to increase from 10 per cent to 25 per cent.
● Favourability had to move from the benchmark score of 58 to at least 70.

- To claim 'material of choice', the thermometer for steel would need to move from last to first place versus its competitors.
- The positive to negative comments ratio had to move from 2:3 to 6:1.

Revisiting metrics

During the campaign, an unexpected measure emerged: 'customers referring to steel in their own advertising'. In the first year, the value of this grew from $1 million to $15 million; by the fifth year, this was worth $128 million.

Review, revise process

The final step concerned reporting the success of the campaign to management, and sending out a monthly newsletter to all stakeholders.

REASSURINGLY EFFECTIVE

Focusing on outcomes rather than outputs means that you automatically avoid relying on ad and brand awareness. These are lesser metrics that in reality offer little substance when it comes to establishing how marketing activity relates to profit.

In the *Journal of Advertising Research*, Heath and Nairn (2005) cite the example of Stella Artois lager, whose ad awareness for its press campaign was tracked by a competitor brand. It had notched up awareness of just 4 per cent, compared with 29 per cent for Castlemaine XXXX. Yet its quality rating was 45 per cent. Heath and Nairn reflect: 'A rigorous analysis of all other factors indicated it could only have been the advertising which gave the brand its exceptionally high repute, thereby confirming that advertising can build strong values without necessarily performing well on memory-based evaluative measures.'

There have been countless studies that examine the variety of ways in which advertising works to influence behaviour. Yet consumers don't necessarily think of ads as having an impact on their behaviour or don't necessarily like crediting them with having such an impact. This is particularly the case when consumers are placed in the artificial situation of being grilled by a market researcher about how much a particular ad has or hasn't influenced their purchasing behaviour.

Instead of marketers tying themselves in knots about how much consumers do or don't recall a particular campaign, a far more constructive way forward is to focus on outcomes. After all, if advertising in the middle of *Who Wants to Be a Millionaire?* sells more fried chicken for KFC, the ad is helping to grow the company's profits. Surely that is the best outcome of all.

6

Forget consumers, target customers

Companies that focus on brand equity place brands on a higher pedestal than customers. Brands are magnets to attract new customers, and anchors to hold existing ones. It must never be forgotten that it is customers, not brands that deliver profits.

Wreden, 2005

Smart investing is about putting your money and efforts into higher-profit, lower-risk opportunities and exploiting your assets. And the single most important asset for any business is its customer base.

When marketers focus on a customer, they can summon up a mental image of who they mean. That customer has a name and a unique set of personal circumstances and product preferences. When marketers think about consumers, there's none of that rich and colourful detail. Instead, there's a faceless crowd of people.

To capture the value from their assets, marketers need to get to know their customers as people. They need to invest not simply in terms of marketing communications, but in terms of the attention that they devote to them. Marketers must be prepared to spend time listening to what customers like and don't like – as well as what they want from the service they receive.

This is how BA created its flat beds, which helped to differentiate its business-class service. Over 48 hours, it listened to 120 of its most loyal customers in a brainstorming session about the future of travel. One of the key findings from the session was that travellers wanted to sleep better, so BA set about delivering the best possible way for them to do so.

Think of a convenience store analogy where the store-owners are friendly and interested in their customers. They remember the details: these customers have a big family so they order the economy-sized packs. The kids have swimming lessons on Thursdays after school, so deliveries need to be after 4.30 pm. Their customers will stay loyal to that store rather than patronizing an alternative where the service may not be as attentive. The reward on the time invested in paying close attention to the comings and goings of everyday family life has the potential to be huge. A family's loyalty to that store could span years, or even decades.

Somewhere along the line in marketing, this sense of intimacy with customers has been lost. That cosy corner-shop closeness that customers once enjoyed is regarded as a thing of the past. Yet with online shopping on the rise, there is in fact more scope than ever to introduce a service-based relationship as a point of difference.

In *People Don't Buy What You Sell, They Buy What You Stand For*, Martin Butler (2005) reminisces about his father retiring after 36 years behind the counter at a hardware shop he owned in Greater London. The local paper ran the headline 'Customers weep as shopkeeper retires' and reported: 'News of Mr Butler's retirement has devastated regular customers – some of whom have been using Butler's Hardware since it opened in 1959 – who describe him as so much more than a shopkeeper, more a friend.'

Successful retailers – whether they are grocers or part of a big retail chain – understand what their customers like and get it for them. They know that, if they keep their customers happy, business will continue to thrive. If they make a mistake, they compensate for it. Crucially, they encourage their staff to behave in exactly the same way. In short, they understand that loyal customers are responsible for keeping them in business, so – just like an investor protecting his or her assets – they strive to look after them.

THE THREE DEADLY SINS...

'Customers' have morphed into a homogeneous mass known as 'consumers' as the following sins have crept into marketing:

1. Pigeon-holing customers into consumer groups segmented by demographics or life stage. This instantly creates a 'them and us' set-up and ignores the simple and universal truth that people prefer to be treated as individuals.
2. Assuming that consumers are fickle and are constantly seeking to switch brands, and then using that assumption to justify concentrating on growth by customer acquisition.
3. Placing more stock on the short-term sale and the value of that sale this quarter rather than assessing long-term loyalty.

When these deadly sins started being committed on a regular basis, marketing began to be consumed by market share rather than being focused on Marketing ROI. This has been detrimental to long-term profits. As *ProfitBrand* states (Wreden, 2005: 3):

> Companies focused on market share see business in terms of competition. As a result, they spend more time trying to out-manoeuvre and out-promote their competition, robbing time and energy from trying to understand customers. Of course, companies must be aware of competitors. But more effort must be spent in learning how competitors are creating and maintaining customer relationships than in trying to 'beat' them.

In the bitterly fought race for market share, marketing has become all about acquiring consumers. This has led to a glut of expensive tactical campaigns, price cuts and trade promotions.

If, as smart companies have realized, the focus shifts to customer retention, marketing's return on investment significantly improves.

Thought leadership often divides a company's key assets into its physical assets (the building, intellectual property, equipment and so on), its people and its brands. Yet there's a much stronger case for arguing that a company's true assets are its customers. In a world characterized by choice, those assets risk being particularly thin on the ground for most companies.

With scant attention being paid to life beyond the next 90 days, companies need to concentrate on laying down the foundations for a long-term relationship with their customers because they are the assets that will provide future shareholder value.

PROFIT (MARKETING ROI) COMES FROM LOYAL CUSTOMERS

I want my marketers to be monitoring customer value rather than customer numbers. Growth marketing is fine, but we tend to focus too much on whether we can recruit rather than retain.

John Sills, Chief Financial Officer, Orange Broadband

If you're still convinced that acquisition is a more lucrative strategy for your organization than focusing on your loyal customers, consider the well-established 80/20 rule in marketing: that 80 per cent of profits are generated by 20 per cent of customers.

As for the other 80 per cent of the consumer base, there's an alarming amount of churn. US businesses lose half of their customers every five years, according to the consultancy Guideline, and some mobile phone companies experience an astonishing customer churn of up to 80 per cent. No wonder so much of their marketing is geared towards acquisition – they're constantly playing catch-up, and have no assets worth protecting.

The consultancy Bain & Company estimates that increasing retention rates by just 5 per cent can potentially increase profits by 25 per cent. Share that statistic with the CEO and the CFO and watch their ears prick up.

As Marketing ROI is a synonym for profit, logic dictates that building loyalty as opposed to acquiring customers is a more profitable strategy for marketing investors. An existing customer who has been satisfied with the experience to date is much more likely to buy another product from you than one who is a total stranger. What's more, tapping into your existing customer base is more cost-efficient when you compare the cost of acquiring and retaining customers. In fact, the average expense of keeping a customer can be as little as one-fifth of the cost of attracting a new one.

A 2004 Deutsche Bank study looked at the effectiveness of TV advertising of 23 packaged goods brands and concluded that only 18 per cent of the advertising generated a positive ROI within a year. In other words, although cash flow increased during that period, it was only for 18 per cent of the time. This is proof that short-term profitability doesn't pay unless there is a more sustaining income stream – and this can come only from a lower-cost repeat purchase – or existing customers continuing to buy a particular product.

To protect their single most important asset, companies should seek to cultivate 'stickability' by shifting their attention to customer retention as opposed to acquisition. It makes much more sense to invest in the closest approximation to the sure-fire thing as opposed to unbalancing the marketing investment portfolio with the risks presented by an acquisition strategy. And, as discussed in Chapter 5, one of the biggest risks associated with acquisition is that new customers who come on board might not offer much in the way of lifetime value, making them cost-inefficient in the long term.

PROFIT (MARKETING ROI) = LOYAL CUSTOMERS

The best strategy that marketing investors can adopt is to focus on building relationships with their customers rather than on counting the number of business transactions they have with them. Imagine it as the difference between a one-night stand and a loving relationship.

A loving relationship entails getting to know your partner. Knowledge intensifies those feelings of love, whereas a one-night stand is a fleeting encounter. The more knowledge that companies can acquire about their current customers – and the more they can use that information when they're communicating with them – the more likelihood they have of building a relationship that will last.

In *Lovemarks* (2004), Kevin Roberts, the Worldwide Chief Executive of Saatchi & Saatchi, argues that love is the holy grail for companies, and even eclipses trust. He writes: 'Think about how you make the most money. You make it when loyal users, heavy users, use your product all the time. That's where the money is.'

He cites examples such as Cheerios – a ring-shaped breakfast cereal that helps little boys to aim when they are potty-training – and Technics decks among the DJing community, which also loves Technics-branded bags, slip mats and T-shirts. These products have built up more than loyalty; they have an active fan base who won't even consider buying anything else.

CUSTOMER SATISFACTION = CUSTOMER RETENTION

Jack Trout makes the following points in his book, *Differentiate or Die: Survival in our era of killer competition* (2000): 1) more than 40 per cent of customers who claimed to be satisfied switched suppliers without looking back; and 2) 89 per cent of people who owned cars from a certain manufacturer said they were very satisfied, and 67 per cent said that they intended to purchase another car from that manufacturer, yet fewer than 20 per cent actually did.

The reasons why a satisfied customer does not stay loyal to a particular brand are that:

1. another company offered a cheaper, more reliable or more efficient service;
2. a trusted source recommended an alternative;
3. when the time came to make a purchasing decision, the customer's satisfaction or loyalty wasn't as concrete as he or she believed it to be.

CUSTOMER EQUITY

Customer equity is the long-term value of a company's customers and represents the asset value of the existing customer base. Customer equity can be an important business metric because it can steer the direction of a company, guiding appropriate customer investments and providing financial measures based on the customers' response to the firm's offerings. Customer equity segments also help a company to develop relevant marketing strategies.

The more your current customers spend, the higher their customer equity becomes. This is the very definition of a virtuous circle. It not only means that your customers are so satisfied that they are putting more business your way; it also has the added benefit of decreasing the need for an acquisition-based strategy to replace 'lost' customers. This makes your marketing communications portfolio much more manageable because you can build a more rounded image of who you're talking to. In turn, this makes it easier to know how best to target your customers and informs what to say when you do, making them more likely to spend money with you.

The customer equity metric

In 1996, Frederick Reichheld, director emeritus and founder of Bain & Company's Loyalty Practice, wrote *The Loyalty Effect: The hidden force behind growth, profits, and lasting value.* In that book, he cited Enterprise Rent-A-Car, Harley-Davidson and the unit trust company Vanguard Group as shining examples of companies that had low cost structures and a strong service ethic. This combination has helped them to become some of the most profitable companies in their sector because they have built up customer equity: fans of their products are highly unlikely to go elsewhere.

Customer equity is a much more reliable benchmark of business success than brand equity because it explains success and failure in business. *The Loyalty Effect* even suggests that relative retention explains profits better than market share, scale, cost, position or any other variable associated with competitive advantage.

And this has been no flash-in-the-pan concept. Thinking around the value of measuring customer equity has become much more sophisticated since *The Loyalty Effect* was first published in 1996. A decade later, we strongly believe that customer equity should be a company's most important metric.

Managing customer equity: five tips

1. Collect accurate data about your customers. Marketers who spell names incorrectly do not deserve to win lifetime loyalty from new customers.
2. Invest in technology and training to make data accessible throughout your organization.
3. Collect acquisition data that offer insights into the typical purchase behaviour of new customers.
4. Track retention over a particular period.
5. Keep tabs on the data. If retention rates fall below 80 per cent, find out where you're losing customers – and act fast.

Customer equity can be defined as the lifetime value of customers discounted by time. As such, it is key to Marketing ROI. Not only does it entail loyal customers who remain committed to a particular product, but it also has value in spreading the gospel: when people like a product, they will recommend it. Businesses that have built up customer equity will also find themselves being forgiven for mistakes much more readily than those that fail to look after their customers. Customers want to be believers, if they are given the opportunity.

Products and services constantly vie for our attention, so loyalty is all about creating such a strong sense of 'pull' towards a particular product that customers don't even reconsider or question their choice. In this scenario, a strong price promotion may change buying habits temporarily, but it will be a blip; customers will not budge their brand choice in the long term, as long as they feel strongly enough about a particular product.

This applies to consumer packaged goods as well as bigger purchases because habit breeds loyalty. Frank Harrison, Strategic Resources Director for ZenithOptimedia Worldwide, makes the point: 'A lot of purchasing is habitual. What percentage of people buy the same brand of toothpaste year in and year out? How easy would it be to convert somebody who's always used a particular brand to start using another? You can only start to judge it when you understand it, and there is not much research in this area.'

Unlike retention, acquiring customers can create costs as opposed to building value. As we discussed in Chapter 5 where we used the example of a credit card company acquiring a new customer, an acquisition-based approach to marketing overlooks actual customer value. Such an organization is, in fact, diluting its own brand, undermining its credibility and missing huge opportunities to increase profitability.

For instance, if a band of loyal customers who have subscribed to a particular service for five years notice that new customers are being treated much better, with more competitive subscription rates and incentives, their loyalty is being abused when it should be rewarded.

Smart marketing investors know that their most loyal customers should always receive preferential treatment because they offer much higher returns.

SEGMENTING BY CUSTOMER PROFITABILITY

Marketers commonly segment their consumers into behavioural or attitudinal groups built from segmentation studies. For instance, a bread company uses descriptors such as 'health vigilantes' or 'casual hedonists' to describe the customer segments it wants to attract. Segmentations such as these provide useful guides that extend beyond demographics and can help influence new product development, packaging and communication.

Identifying unprofitable customers

Just as stock market investors weed out the underperforming investments in their portfolios, marketing investors need to perform exactly the same task by segmenting their customers in terms of their profitability.

One advantage of segmentation is that it not only allows profitable customers to be identified and targeted, but it also allows companies to see which customers are more trouble than they're worth.

John Sills at Orange Broadband says:

> Forty per cent of our customers don't want anything other than fast internet access, so we segment the market between those who want a £14.99 a month product – and who actually make us very little profit – and those who are replacing their phone line with one of our fixed line phones and installing video-on-demand services. In the future, it is those products that will make money for Orange Broadband, so we divide up our communications budget in proportion to the increased contribution we get from customers in those areas.

Unprofitable customers are bad news. They don't generate any profits for the company and they drain resources, sapping the workforce's precious time and energy.

Case study: Capital One – 'Love 'ems' and 'kill yous' strategy for success

In the 1980s, the credit card company Capital One noticed that competitive banks were charging all their customers the same interest rates, regardless of their short- or long-term profitability. So it took a different tack altogether.

Having undertaken some customer equity analysis, Capital One identified two primary segments in its customer base: profitable customers were 'love 'ems', while 'kill yous' were unprofitable.

The company decided to pursue the 'love 'ems' and charge them less than their current credit card provider. (The 'kill yous', in the meantime, could drain the resources of Capital One's competitors.)

The strategy pivoted on encouraging balance transfers to a credit card with a lower annual percentage rate than the going rate. Those customers – the 'love 'ems' – who had a credit card balance where switching to Capital One would save them money every month jumped ship. They saved money on their monthly payments, while Capital One benefited from their current – and their future – business.

Two decades later, Capital One continues to use information on its customers to grow its business. For instance, it anticipates callers who phone up to check their balance every month, so it has made a balance check the first option for these callers. The company also exploits the selling opportunity by knowing the next most likely product for this customer. Capital One's best sales reps will sell new products to 15 per cent of incoming callers.

Other examples of brands that have successfully used segmentation include Gordon's gin. The Diageo brand attracts younger customers by advertising to them, but retains older drinkers through direct marketing.

Customer profitability has a direct line of sight to corporate profitability. By concentrating on retaining customers rather than acquiring them, you are driving long-term profitability. You're also guarding your best assets and practising focus investing (see Chapter 10).

Segmenting by customer profitability

Fred Reichheld (2001) says that one reason why companies have become so obsessed with acquiring customers as opposed to retaining them is because acquisition is much easier to measure. He comments:

The sad truth is that customer acquisition is easier to measure and to reward than building loyal relationships. It is easy to attribute new customers to the salesman, the new product, or the marketing campaign, while turning customers into promoters is everyone's job (and therefore, no one's job). This is why it is so important to hold teams accountable; just as accountable as they now feel for generating accounting profits.

It is worth investing in segmentation tools that divide up your customers according to their profitability. Crudely splitting up your consumer base into 'loyal' and 'new' limits how far you can go based on that information. Yet if you segment using a more sophisticated tool based on customer profitability, you can allocate your resources accordingly, reducing servicing and acquisition costs for unprofitable customers, while adding and enhancing value for more profitable ones.

This offers advantages throughout your organization, not least for employees. They can see just by glancing at a computer screen which customers fall into the 'most profitable' segments and act accordingly. This insight enables them to improve the customization of the service available with the intention of providing better customer satisfaction and responsiveness. It also has benefits for the organization's customer acquisition strategy: customers who are with rival brands catch glimpses of the service that loyal customers receive with your organization and want a piece of the action.

The 3Rs: three steps to segmenting by customer profitability

1. *Ranking.* Create a scale of 1 to 10 where you can rank your entire customer base in terms of their profitability. You can use sales volume, margin or length of tenure as your metric, but your ranking will ideally be based on profitability of costs allocated to customers versus revenue gained from them. Once ranked, prioritize your highest-value customers and invest in them. Develop segment profiles that note purchasing patterns, media habits and demographics. This information will help inform and influence your marketing communications strategy.
2. *Relevance.* Target different ranks with the most appropriate offers. Think of the different types of customer on the same jumbo jet heading for the same destination on the same plane. There are first-class, business, premium-economy and economy customers and each segment has different priorities: for some it's comfort and for others it's getting the cheapest possible seat. You need to cultivate a similar approach when you create customer offerings, if you are going to increase the likelihood of surpassing your customers' expectations and retaining them for future business. Forrester Research reveals that only 43 per cent of 60 global companies offer better service to profitable customers, so there is a lot of scope for improvement.
3. *Reshape.* Based on the information that you accumulate about your customers, develop an understanding of the different ways in which your customers are acquired. Do they join up via the internet, through existing customers or via telemarketing? How does it differ according to their profile? Armed with this information, you can ensure that you

invest more heavily in marketing that delivers high-profit customers as well as reducing or even stopping those executions that don't. This delivers much more efficient and productive communication. More data and a more insightful understanding will gently steer your business towards attracting 'love 'ems' rather than 'kill yous'.

The 3Rs help to tailor your customer service and marketing investment and steer organizations away from a 'one size fits all' approach. Segmenting by customer profitability allows marketers to match the service and the marketing effort in a much more fiscally responsible way.

Maximizing customer profitability

Once a customer base has been segmented by profitability, there are 10 steps to maximizing customer profitability, according to Blattberg and Deighton (1996):

1. Invest in high-value customers first.
2. Transform product management into customer management. This can mean creating a club that offers high-value customers certain benefits and that reinforces the brand's appeal. Blattberg and Deighton cite Harley-Davidson, Nintendo and Lego as examples.
3. Consider increasing customer equity through additional sales and cross-selling.
4. Reduce acquisition costs. If you can acquire customers in a more cost-efficient way, the long-term pay-off from those customers improves. Many virtual brands have low acquisition costs because they are part of affiliation marketing schemes. Similarly, customer referrals, where existing customers are incentivized for introducing new customers, are cost-effective.
5. Track customer equity gains and losses against marketing programmes.
6. Use customer-value statement reports to find out whether marketing is building or eroding the customer base (for more information on tracking investments, turn to Chapter 11).
7. Relate branding to customer equity (not the other way around).
8. Monitor the retainability of your customers. Has anything in their circumstances changed that might make them less inclined to purchase from your product portfolio?
9. Consider separating acquisition and retention marketing strategies.

10. Remember: when managers strive to grow customer equity, they put the customer at the forefront of their strategic thinking.

Marketing communication strategies to increase customer profitability

Some organizations have so many silos and fiefdoms that marketing risks becoming all about customer acquisition, while retention remains the exclusive property of the account management and service teams. The case for ripping down cultural barriers between departments has never been stronger.

Brand communication is the cumulative number of touchpoints of the company; it's not just a big budget ad campaign on TV, or a direct marketing mail-out. A consumer engages with a company via a call centre, a product's performance, an experience of a service, or interaction with the sales team. And there are many more touchpoints besides. For example, one of the major touchpoints a bank has with its customers – and even non-customers too – is its ATM machines. It is puzzling that so few banks use these machines to appeal to different segments within their customer base. Marketing can seize on opportunities through all of these touchpoints to enhance a customer's experience of an organization, with the endgame being to retain that customer over several years. When touchpoints are handled appropriately, other factors can serve to reinforce a customer's brand choice.

The investment management company Vanguard Group invests just 10–15 per cent of what its competitors spend on communications spending. Yet it has grown 30 per cent annually. The secret of its success? PR, advertising and direct mail communications are all focused on reinforcing the purchase decisions of its existing customer base. All of its efforts are based on customer retention by informing them about new products and reinforcing previous purchase decisions.

CUSTOMER RETENTION HELPS ACQUISITION

Fred Reichheld, in his *Harvard Business Review* article 'The one number you need to grow' (2003), suggests that there is one specific metric that is particularly useful: willingness for existing customers to recommend a particular product or service to a friend, family member or colleague. He has christened this metric 'the ultimate question'.

When advocacy is matched with a brand's ability to empathize with its consumer base, marketers have hit upon a potent combination. Teenage girls, for instance, love to share information and help their friends, and P&G leverages this on its beinggirl websites for the femcare brands Always and Tampax. The sites take a big-sister approach that appeals to the holistic well-being of girls and includes 'advice for life', beauty tips and fun activities. If the consumer being targeted has positive associations about these products when she's a teenager, she's much more likely to use them in the decades to come.

Better insight leads to appropriate offers being sensibly timed, and this improves the chances of customer take-up. For instance, when a credit cardholder gets married, card companies offer an incentive to the spouse-to-be to become a joint cardholder. Such gestures require minimal effort on the part of the marketer, yet can generate a maximum reward in the form of a new customer for life.

Case study: Tesco – Personalized marketing through Clubcard

Tesco's Clubcard in the UK has become the granddaddy of all loyalty schemes, giving the supermarket a special place in the hearts and minds of its customers: a Millward Brown brand loyalty study reveals that Tesco remains the supermarket with which consumers feel the most affinity.

Clubcard helped Tesco to create this culture of affinity by amassing a wealth of information about its customers through the scheme. What's more, it uses the data wisely. Clubcard tracks £4 out of every £5 spent at the shop. Clubcard's impact became clear a year after Tesco introduced the scheme: Clubcard holders were spending 28 per cent more at Tesco and 16 per cent less in Sainsbury's.

Launched in 1995, the scheme rewards Tesco customers for each £1 spent with Tesco and Clubcard partners. When members have earned a minimum of 150 points, the points are converted into vouchers, which are mailed out to Clubcard holders and which are redeemable with Tesco and branded partners, and for air miles.

Today, 13 million customers receive this quarterly mailing, which is heavily segmented so that customers receive offers that are most appropriate to them. There are 1 million different targeted offers, but each one is designed to drive incremental sales. Some £100 million in incremental sales is generated through response rates that average 25–30 per cent.

Through its Clubcard, Tesco builds up a shopping history of each and every cardholder, which helps the retailer to make its customer communications relevant. This has translated into the online space where shoppers can go to tesco.com and see a list of all the purchases that they have made in the last three months. Here, Clubcard holders can also take advantage of offers for other, similar products at special prices.

Case study: Southwest Airlines – Really putting the customer first

Following 9/11, Southwest Airlines, one of the United States' largest domestic carriers, agreed to give refunds to all customers who asked for them. On the day of the attacks, the company issued a dignified statement, which included the words: 'All Southwest Airlines customers with a confirmed reservation can request a full refund from Southwest regardless of travel date.' In the event, very few came forward to claim their money back, but the fact that Southwest Airlines' very first thought had been with its customers marked it out as a brand that cared deeply about people.

At a difficult time for the United States and the airline industry, Southwest wanted to make sure that its customers felt looked after by the brand. Its insistence on offering refunds shows how well a marketing strategy can align with a customer-centric business strategy.

A news release distributed just two weeks after 9/11, on 25 September, urged flyers 'Let's keep moving forward', and offered customers heavily subsidized fares, including a $34 round trip ticket between Los Angeles and Las Vegas.

At the time, Joyce Rogge, Southwest's Senior Vice President of Marketing, commented: 'We are determined to get back to business. The 32,000 employees of Southwest Airlines together salute the American spirit, and we stand with our fellow airlines in the mission to get America flying again.'

Since 2001, the airline has bucked the trend and remained profitable; many other domestic carriers in the United States have not hit the right tone with their marketing and offered customers ill-timed benefits such as extra legroom and in-flight services. Southwest, with its more human approach, managed to strike exactly the right chord with its customers and consequently reaped the rewards: it has been profitable for 33 consecutive years.

Case study: O2 – Keeping customers, growing profits

Mobile phone networks have historically treated customer relationships like flings; they woo you with flowers and chocolates and don't care about you afterwards. We want to be more about the long-term relationship rather than the fling.

Susie Moore,
UK Head of Brand and Marketing Communications, O2

As in all countries where mobile phone penetration has grown rapidly over the last decade, there has been a scramble by the operators in the UK to steal each other's customers through acquisition-based strategies. The seven brands offered little differentiation other than price, brand and service.

Customer satisfaction levels were plummeting as existing customers became disillusioned with all the brands. Customers regarded the operators as 'being all the same', putting all their energies into acquiring new customers while neglecting their existing ones.

O2 was no exception. Its churn rate hit 35 per cent in 2004. So it decided to rewrite the rule book.

O2 decided to put its customer at the heart of everything and to reward loyalty. It made operational improvements and began to offer existing customers the same deals as new customers. For instance, pre-pay customers were offered 10 per cent off top-ups every three months, while contract customers were offered 50 per cent extra airtime on their bundle for life when they renewed their contract exclusively with O2.

An integrated campaign by its ad agency VCCP centred around the message: 'O2: a world that revolves around you'. In addition to TV, outdoor, press, point of sale, web, e-mail marketing and postcards, O2 also began using text messages to talk to its customers, offering rewards as 'presents' where all the customer had to do was to text back a number.

By December 2005, O2 had the largest UK user base of any network and hadn't sustained any loss in average revenue. Responses via text were unprecedented – hitting over 50 per cent.

Modelling showed that pre-pay churn rate reduced by over a third, while contract reduced by over a tenth. It also indicated that, if the new strategy hadn't been introduced, O2's churn rate would have nudged 40 per cent and would have been the highest in the marketplace. Econometric analysis showed that 1 million disconnections were prevented by the campaign.

Over a period of three to four years, the estimated payback of the campaign was 80 times the advertising investment.

CONSUMER PACKAGED GOODS

In an article entitled 'Why are fmcgs going below the line?' by Claire Billings published by *Campaign* on 9 June 2006, Hamish Torrie, Brand Equity Champion for Ardbeg whisky, Glenmorangie, commented:

> We've launched products and built a brand from nothing to tens of thousands of cases in six years with our CRM programme. It's not just a question of having a nice, fluffy relationship; there's a win for members because they get first access to anything we do, which makes them feel respected by the brand. It's about having a personal relationship, but you can't fake these things, it's got to be genuine.

Most customers of consumer packaged goods are less locked into a single brand; they tend to be repertoire buyers who demonstrate very little brand loyalty.

This makes segmentation more important in the consumer packaged goods sector. Indeed, clever targeting provides a firm foundation for packaged goods brands to promote loyalty and repeat use.

Big consumer packaged goods advertisers – who used to be faithful users of mass media – are now starting to realize the value of talking directly with their customers. In the UK, for instance, Nestlé has developed customer relationship management strategies for its brands, including a £15 million loyalty scheme.

THE POWER OF EMPATHY

Climbing into the skin of your customer can generate considerable gains. If you can anticipate customers' moods and when and what they want to buy, you will start noticing a return. Bruce Springsteen fans had this experience via Ticketmaster. After buying gig tickets online, they received communications both before and after the show: beforehand, they had information on pre-concert events, views of the stage from their seats and e-mail updates of the tour. Afterwards, they received an e-mail from Springsteen, a concert playlist and links to buy CDs and other merchandise. The day-after e-mails generated a 47 per cent response rate.

Meanwhile in the Netherlands, ING Bank teamed up with SPSS, a worldwide predictive analytics software and solutions provider, to create a credit offer. If customers visited an ATM in the Netherlands to withdraw cash and were told that they had insufficient funds, ING checked their credit rating and, if appropriate, would mail them a credit offer within the next few days. The response rate exceeded 50 per cent.

In China, Procter & Gamble embarked on an e-mail marketing campaign for Head & Shoulders. The shampoo brand was already a massive hit in the country – in fact, China is its biggest market. It managed to capitalize further on its popularity by inviting users to refer a friend, using a Head & Shoulders sample as an incentive. In many Western markets, because of the stigma associated with having dandruff, this referral system would never have taken off, but in China it was simply regarded as caring about a friend's problem. The campaign received an outstanding response.

BESPOKE MEDIA

An increasingly common way to promote customer loyalty through communication is to launch a customer magazine. Service brands are particularly fond of magazines, and BA, one of our Marketing ROI stars, has one of the best known, *High Life*, which has been on BA planes since

1973. BA also publishes a second title, which primarily targets short-haul customers, *Business Life*. Both adhere to high design and production values and are geared towards enhancing the flying experience.

Retailers also find magazines a particularly effective way to promote products and to communicate with their customers. Publicis Blueprint works with the UK department store Debenhams on its magazine, *Desire*. According to Blueprint, looking at the magazine tempts 50 per cent of readers to buy a product. As *Desire* has a circulation of 745,126 (July–December 2005), this can potentially offer a seriously impressive ROI.

Publicis Blueprint also worked with the finance department at Debenhams to help promote those parts of the store that tend to be neglected by shoppers because of their location. The toiletries department, for instance, had a much stronger footfall than the hair salon or the café because it was on the ground floor rather than the top floor. The magazine worked hard to increase the average spend per customer – £70 – by showcasing other departments to customers and encouraging them to visit. Jason Frost, the Managing Director of Publicis Blueprint, comments: 'It's about making the best possible use of the store's existing customer base, which in Debenhams' case is the tens of millions of customers who are either store cardholders or who pick up the magazine in-store. The secret to customer loyalty is communication and giving your customers something that they value.'

USE THE TECHNOLOGY TO GUIDE SMART INVESTMENTS

Giant leaps in media and database-management mean that there are many more opportunities for advertisers to use personal data to improve communications with their customers. Data can steer them back towards the 'customer' relationship of old rather than an impersonal 'consumer' relationship.

Your most loyal customers are your best assets. To make your marketing portfolio work, these assets need to be protected above everything else.

7

Manage your communication investment portfolio

Intuitively and intellectually, I believe that marketing delivers ROI. But the thing I always struggle with is the relative success in ROI of different activities and how you measure and compare each one. That's the main issue in terms of allocating your available spend in the most optimal fashion.

Ian Edwards, Finance Director, Comet Group

YOUR MARKETING COMMUNICATION PORTFOLIO

Any big investment decisions in marketing communication can be distilled into three questions:

1. How much should you invest?
2. Where and how should you deploy your budget?
3. What messages will you communicate?

This chapter will focus on how to deal with the questions of where and how you should invest your marketing communication.

Advertising agencies see themselves as part of a creative industry. They exist to support clients' businesses, but first and foremost their culture and focus are defined by producing ads and communication. Creativity shapes their identity and success, and it's been that way for decades. For this reason, much of the initial advertising planning hones in on the development of the message.

From an investment point of view, however, there's a case for arguing that it's far more constructive to start with identifying *where* you want your funds to be deployed. Then – and only then – should you turn your attention to the message itself.

Marketers and their agencies can benefit from adopting a broader portfolio approach to their marketing investments. That way, they can properly consider the wide range of options available to them rather than being too hemmed in by an over-reliance on one particular channel – as has historically been the case with 30-second TV ads. This portfolio approach enables both marketers and agencies to think much more strategically about the 'how' rather than the 'what' element in marketing communications.

Where the budget is deployed is a critical strategic decision and can form a differentiating element of a strategy. For instance, *The Economist*'s famous 'red on white' executions predominantly use posters, giving it stand-out, while Absolut vodka has traditionally spent a generous half of its marketing budget on iconic press ads. Based on their commitment to one particular medium alone, both campaigns have more than proved their stamina. The decision about where to invest has been critical to their success and extremely well managed by the respective portfolio managers at the Economist Group and Absolut.

EMBRACING RISK

Budget allocation is a key investment decision that is linked to Marketing ROI, and in most cases it's an area that is ripe for improvement. Many marketers have a worrying tendency to fall into the trap of sticking with the same plan year after year. Despite investing time and energy in consulting their agencies and reviewing their investments, an aversion to risk kicks in.

Yet ask any stock market investor and he or she will say that managing an investment portfolio involves knowing how to manage risk. The same goes for the successful management of a marketing communications portfolio. It is only by managing risk that a marketing communications investor will learn how to reduce it. By the same token, if marketers fail to evolve their portfolio there is actually far more risk attached to this inertia in the long term than fostering a more adventurous approach. Developing a healthy attitude towards risk is part and parcel of being a serious investor who is committed to generating profit. Yet many marketers remain steadfast in their commitment to last year's decisions.

Pat Fallon, Chairman of Fallon, commented to *Contagious* magazine in June 2006: 'In the US, people now spend up to 20 per cent of their media consumption time on new technology channels – everything from cell phones to games to the internet. But marketers are still spending 90 per cent of their money on old media.'

A DIFFERENT APPROACH

By 'managing your marketing communications investment portfolio', we are encouraging a different approach. Instead of relying entirely on judgement, bottom-up planning, agency pitches or how you've allocated your funds in the past, we are suggesting that your portfolio should be proactively managed. As part of this approach, we recommend integrating all the elements of the marketing promotion mix. This includes not just broadcast media, print, outdoor and direct, but also in-store, branded content and events.

By re-evaluating your portfolio, you will gain a greater opportunity to improve your overall marketing communication strategy and you will strengthen your chances of generating more impressive profits.

This four-step approach will assist you in making an integrated approach payback because it exactly matches how a fund manager regards his or her own investment portfolio:

- *Step one: Identify the bankers.* According to investment analysts, 80 per cent of an investor's return is about choosing the right markets and sectors as opposed to individual company stocks or shares. An investor must decide which sectors are the most promising in exactly the same way that a marketing director has to determine which channels will work most appropriately. We believe that selecting the right channels contributes to at least half of the result.

    There's often a tendency to overemphasize the implementation strategies of one particular investment at the expense of determining the overall mix. The latter is influenced either by science or by intuition, and it is frequently steered by advice from the agencies' recommendations.

- *Step two: Determine how much to allocate in each channel.* You need to choose channels depending on how much influence on purchase each one will have. We advocate a more selective approach, which focuses on fewer channels, but this decision will ultimately be led by communication goals.
- *Step three: Constantly review your portfolio.* As with the stock market, the performances of marketing channels vary over time, so marketing investors constantly need to review how their portfolios are performing. In this chapter, we offer tools to help marketers review their decisions to help them assess whether they need to make changes.
- *Step four: Leverage synergies.* This is about making all of your marketing investments work together seamlessly. For investors, once the sectors are chosen their job becomes all about picking the best stocks. For marketing investors, the channel-planning process involves choosing the best possible combination of channels. Their selection is based on the investment objectives of the overall plan, insight from consumers, data analysis and efficiency to drive the optimum cost. A great deal of this information usually comes from their stockbrokers or, in marketing's case, their agency partners.

THE INTEGRATION CHALLENGE

In the United States, the Association of National Advertisers (ANA) and Blueprint Communications Inc collaborated on a research study conducted in 2006 that highlighted marketers' disappointment with integration. Canvassing opinion among ANA members, the survey found that only a third of advertisers rated their integrated marketing communication as 'excellent' or 'very good'. More worryingly, a third of those surveyed rated it as 'poor' or 'fair'. One telecommunications marketing manager lamented: 'There are so many different communications disciplines and lines of business that it is difficult to coordinate and pull it together.'

The consensus was that, while integration was a great idea in theory, in practice it was extremely difficult to achieve. One vice-president of marketing services for a materials manufacturer observed: 'Getting everyone on the same page is a real challenge.'

Yet it's not impossible. British Airways historically used to employ three different touchpoints – TV, print and outdoor. When it launched its comeback campaign in 2002, it used 10, including ATMs, branded content and online. Coordinating a larger collection of touchpoints was undoubtedly more challenging for BA's roster of agencies, but it paid dividends: the campaign helped to revitalize the carrier and reverse its sales decline.

Online has meant a huge change in how BA operates. Woody Harford, BA's Senior Vice President Commercial in North America, claims that over four times as many interact with BA via ba.com rather than via airports.

The reasons why integration is hard to implement

- *The silo factor.* Marketing departments are often split into specialist departments such as media, sponsorship and digital.
- *Expertise.* The task of coordinating different channel disciplines and lines of business is eminently challenging. What's more, in-house marketing staff and agencies may have certain agendas to which they insist on clinging; their department is used to handling a particular discipline and they have built up experience within it.
- *A lack of common metrics.* Each discipline will have its own means of measuring effectiveness, so metrics will differ. A direct marketing campaign, for instance, will be measured in cost per response, whereas sponsorship will measure awareness and press coverage. In some media, such as viral marketing, the investments are so negligible that they don't justify the huge expense involved in measuring their effectiveness. There is no consistent format to measure and evaluate across channels. Existing research favours certain solutions such as awareness measurement for TV advertising.
- *Agency culture.* Despite often boasting it on their credentials, few agencies can genuinely work across different channels. The ANA/Blueprint report concluded: 'Marketers are less likely to turn to full-service agencies to provide integrated services than they are to combine an advertising agency with separate firms that specialize in promotion, event marketing, direct response, public relations and Internet communications.'

    In reality, agencies have shrunk. Once they used to provide a 'full service' experience for their clients, but today, as clients have reduced their margins and opted for fees over commission, these services have been reduced. This has led to specialist shops profiting from marketers who plump for the *à la carte* rather than the *prix fixe* option.

In truth, only a handful of agencies can work well collaboratively. Typically, an ad agency wants to take the lead over other specialist companies and doesn't want to cede control of the strategy to another agency because it doesn't want to lose any income attached to a particular account. Yet all agencies share a desire to be centre-stage. Woody Harford remembers trying to coordinate nine marketing agencies when BA in the United States first started experimenting with digital media. He recalls: 'Managing so many agencies was a burden because every agency wants to feel like they're your core marketing partner.'

Mark Ritson from the London Business School commented in *Marketing* on 22 November 2002: 'The fanfare that greeted the emergence of integrated marketing communications in the early 1990s has died away, leaving the industry uncomfortably aware that it still represents a series of one trick ponies.' He believes that only the client can drive integration, although he adds that few clients have the skills and the resources to do this effectively.

The leadership question

US companies that participated in the ANA/Blueprint study regretted that their agencies weren't as involved as they wanted them to be because they considered them to be the 'best source' for integrated marketing communications. One marketing executive for a consumer packaged goods company even felt moved to comment: 'Very few ad agency people can talk intelligently across all the marketing communications vehicles and disciplines.'

In this scenario, marketers face two choices: they can either take the one-stop-shop route or they can enlist the help of specialists. The problem with the latter is that specialists tend to be entrepreneurial operations that can be blinkered to the bigger picture. What's more, they demand tighter management; each one will work in a different way and to a different timetable, which can present logistical headaches. As Amy O'Kane, BA's VP Marketing Communications, North America, asks: 'How much do you get involved with managing your different agencies and encouraging them to play nicely together in the sandbox?'

Yet the one-stop-shop route is no guarantee for a stress-free life either. The trend for holding company pitches around 2004 had many industry experts claiming that 'super-pitches' might be the future for global corporations. Yet delivery on accounts that have been decided at holding company rather than at individual agency level has been patchy at best. Rishad Tobaccowala, the CEO of digital consultancy Denuo, observes: 'Clients aren't looking for a one-stop shop. They outsource almost every other thing that they do, so why would they say "I'm putting all my money with you" when it comes to communications?'

The answer...

We believe that collaboration – steered by strong client leadership – is the answer. When it comes to communication portfolio management, the buck should stop with marketing or brand directors. Therefore, it's entirely appropriate that they should be responsible from the outset for any decisions regarding their agencies as advisers and consultants.

Any investor seeks out help, support and counsel by asking stock-brokers and consulting tip sheets and financial advisers. But when decisions have to be made, the money being spent doesn't belong to those who have offered their pearls of wisdom; they will not reap the benefits or suffer the consequences. It's the same with marketing. Most remuneration structures don't reward performance, so agencies don't have a stake in whether their advice has worked or not for their clients. As the ultimate responsibility falls on clients' shoulders, it's logical that they should own their decision making, but at the same time they should encourage collaboration among their agency collective.

The collaboration conundrum

The next hurdle is fostering a collaborative spirit between different agencies.

One of our Marketing ROI stars makes no secret about its desire for agencies to work more collaboratively. Bernhard Glock, the Manager of Global Media and Communication at Procter & Gamble, comments:

> If agencies could collaborate more effectively, we would see greater holistic communications across all our brands in all countries. One agency alone is not capable of being best in class. There are different ways to

organize collaboration. But there's no doubt that the stronger the part-nership, the stronger the relationship of the team and the more it can leverage the diversity of different personalities and talents.

Marketing directors must manage, properly fund and resource lead-ership on integrated marketing communications strategy and evalu-ation, rather than allow it to be led from the bottom up. If they don't, they risk finding themselves caught in the crossfire between their different marketing specialists.

The portfolio approach

Within the marketing department too, someone must own integration. Specialists are required to produce materials, but communication gener-alists are needed to plan and manage an integrated communications programme.

Companies have experimented with employing strategy consultants, media agencies and integrated agencies in addition to their full-service agency. A communication management agency has up to four remits:

1. taking responsibility for leading or supporting the brand manager and the communications programme from a planning point of view;
2. handling routine executions internally;
3. building relationships with specialist agencies that can provide communication expertise;
4. monitoring the work of specialist agencies to check that they remain on brief.

Case study: O2 – 'It only works if it all works'

O2 is famous for its distinctive bubbles on a calming blue background, elements that appear on all of its marketing communications.

Susie Moore, O2's UK Head of Brand and Marketing Communications, comments: 'The O2 bubbles and their philosophy – that O2 gives you the oxygen to communicate – is all about being completely consistent.'

She adds: 'Internally, our motto was "It only works if it all works" and that came about by being true to the brand through every single touchpoint. It sounds obvious, but not everyone does it, and it's been key to our success. Every single message we give customers is consistent.'

This is integration in action, facilitated by collaboration across all of O2's agencies, and led by VCCP, O2's ad agency.

VCCP takes the lead from both a brand and a point-of-sale point of view, yet it also encourages and incorporates input from agency partners such as the media agency ZenithOptimedia, the direct agency Archibald Ingall Stretton, and Agency Republic, O2's digital agency.

VCCP is a new breed of agency. On launching, two of its founding principles were: 'Be un-precious' and 'Be informal.' Both these principles stand it in good stead in terms of offering the truly collaborative approach to integration that many clients seek.

Another Marketing ROI star, P&G, has made changes to reflect a more holistic approach. In the United States, it appointed its first ever VP of Marketing in North America, to lead its total marketing efforts. In the UK, P&G operates an agency process that involves briefing and integrating all its marketing partners with a view to developing and delivering holistic strategies.

GROWTH OF ALTERNATIVE CHANNELS TO ADVERTISING

Media advertising's share of marketing budgets in the United States has almost halved in the last 25 years. In 1976, it was 42 per cent of the spend; by 2002, this had fallen to 24 per cent. Meanwhile, trade and consumer promotions have both increased.

Similarly, advertising in media grew by just 0.7 per cent between 2001 and 2004 in the world's biggest advertising markets: the United States, Japan, the UK, Germany and France. Advertising is losing share of the total marketing budget to other areas of marketing expenditure, most notably interactive marketing, which, over the same time period, grew by nearly 30 per cent.

These statistics come from the *Marketing Expenditure Trends Report*, which is written by Patrick Barwise and Alan Styler and is published annually by the London Business School. The data are based on interviews with over 900 chief marketing officers in all five countries. The 2003 report concluded: 'Direct, especially interactive, marketing (which is defined as all forms of online and one-to-one activity) will continue to grow at the expense of traditional media advertising for the foreseeable future.'

There is a growing need to recognize the mounting competition for marketing budgets, particularly from more measurable and accountable interactive routes to market. Advertisers are seeking a measurable return from their marketing investment, not just in 'soft' metrics such as brand equity and tracking scores, but also in the 'hard' measures of brand profit and sales.

Yet the success of TV as an advertising medium was built largely on the back of its ability to brand-build, a function that doesn't cut much ice in the new economy. One of the issues confronting TV companies is a need to demonstrate the effect of advertising on sales. If they don't, TV will lose out to media that are more easily measurable.

Diversifying beyond traditional media

Media advertising remains an important component in the marketing communication portfolio, but there are increasingly more options to increase returns from your marketing mix. With the shift to more holistic communications, the question has shifted from 'Where do I advertise?' to 'How should I advertise?'

The need to invest in a portfolio management approach has emerged from marketers' requirements to achieve more than awareness building. Alternative communication channels are emerging all the time, offering marketers new opportunities to talk to consumers and create differentiated experiences. Many of these channels at the moment are niche targeting opportunities, so a marketing investor needs to find the right combination of engagement and experience in combination with higher reach to achieve multiple objectives. The portfolio approach gives the marketing investor a mechanism for centrally managing an ever-increasing number of touchpoints.

An on-demand world

Consumers' ability to dodge ads and advertisers' rediscovery of engagement mean that traditional media are not the only choice. All indications agree that consumers are gravitating towards on-demand media: ZenithOptimedia Group estimates that, in 2005, around 6 per cent of US homes had a DVR, and that number is on an upward curve. What's more, eMarketer figures show that video on demand is available in 12 per cent of US homes, broadband is in 23 per cent and portable DVD players are in 19 per cent. The idea of sitting down to watch a programme scheduled for a specific time and broadcast on networked TV is already becoming quaint.

The TV networks are fighting back by acquiring online properties – for instance News Corporation's purchase of online community hub MySpace – and are being more active in packaging branded content, digital, sponsorship and other owned properties to give marketers more integrated and experience-driven communications from the seller's end.

This means that the explosion of new choices – traditional niche media that are becoming wider-reaching and more economic to deploy – presents a veritable selection box for any advertiser seeking an integrated approach to marketing investment. Digital, events and product placement specialists have become much more sophisticated, accountable and financially viable for marketers. As a result, there is far more experimentation taking place.

Marketers must test new channels and new media by actively allocating up to 20 per cent of the budget for experimentation. As traditional advertising cedes share to more interactive, personal, experiential and – ultimately – measurable channels, the need for marketers to be able to apply the principles of investment to an ever-growing portfolio of touchpoints will intensify. One of those principles is feeling at ease about a comfortable level of risk taking.

PAYBACK TIME

It's worth making the time to plan how to handle a marketing communication investment portfolio, because investing in integration pays back. When consumers are receiving a consistent message *à la* O2, the messages reinforce each other and have more chance of striking a chord with consumers.

Case study: Unilever – 'Make Luv with Lynx'

One brand that provides a compelling case on the power of integration is Unilever's Axe brand, which is known as Lynx in the UK, Ireland and Australia.

In 2003, Lynx's agency, Bartle Bogle Hegarty, didn't want to do 'just another ad' to promote Pulse, its new variant. Instead, it set out to create a phenomenon, a story outlined by Nicholls and Raillard (2004).

It hooked the launch into the dance music track 'Make Luv' by Room 5, and developed a series of choreographed moves that could be copied in clubs. The agency Dare Digital, then created 'The Dotman', an animated character created from the dots on Pulse's packaging, which performed the dance online. A TV ad and PR campaign followed, while dancers and student brand managers took the moves on to club dance floors on Friday nights.

'Make Luv' shot to number one in the UK and stayed there for four weeks, selling over 325,000 copies. The ad scored highly on recognition and word-of-mouth scores and generated stacks of PR.

In France and Spain – which are regarded as good control markets for Lynx – an integrated campaign wasn't in operation. The results for the Pulse launch weren't as impressive. In France, the launch was heralded by TV and print advertising, while in Spain only below-the-line channels were launched.

According to figures from Information Resources, ACNielsen and Unilever's then media agency, Initiative, Lynx Pulse sold 1,457,586 cans in France in 2003 on a communication investment of €2.34 million, giving a cost of €1.60 per can sold. Yet in the UK, 12,773,000 cans of Pulse were sold in the same time period on a communication investment of €4.71 million. Each can sold cost just €0.37, so France spent 4.3 times as much money per can of Lynx Pulse as the UK. Spain delivered a negative sales effect.

In an IPA Effectiveness Paper about Lynx Pulse from 2004, *Proving the Value of Integration*, two planners at BBH, Will Nicholls and Gwen Raillard, who worked on the Lynx account, commented: 'Launching a new variant by creating a phenomenon around it with integrated communication is more efficient than other approaches. Integrated multichannel campaigns can be more than twice as efficient at generating a return than advertising-only solutions. Every euro invested in an

> integrated campaign should work at least twice as hard as a euro
> invested in advertising-only campaigns.'
> *Source*: IPA Effectiveness Awards, WARC.

Channel planning

Different media prompt a range of consumer responses. To generate immediate response for a sale, high-reaching traditional mass media will communicate that message effectively and quickly. Yet as they grow in sophistication, the primary role of a medium can change. The internet started out as a strong response channel. But now that bandwidth has increased, it has evolved into a broadcast medium too: video trailers and short films are broadcast online and TV networks sell episodes of hit shows via broadband connections.

It's not just online that benefits from advances in technology. P&G in the UK pioneered the use of outdoor Hypertag technology to initiate sampling for its haircare product Aussie 3 Minute Miracle. The posters invited consumers to activate the infrared on their mobile and point it at the Hypertag contained in the poster. The consumer received a unique key code and a text prompt for aussiehair.com, as well as the chance to win a trip to Australia.

MAKING THE RIGHT INVESTMENT DECISIONS

When you consider your entire portfolio, you will want to evaluate, compare, select and switch different marketing channels. Here are four tips for making the right decisions:

1. *Focus investment in channels that deliver proven Marketing ROI.* Don't waste time trying to make channels work; stick to the 'winners'. Align your marketing goals with your business objectives and establish priorities and plans at corporate, business, brand and consumer segment level. Return to the ICE checklist in Chapter 4 and keep asking yourself what you are trying to achieve.
2. *Go for channel neutrality.* Be prepared to switch channels. Tracking technology – particularly for digital campaigns – allows you to make changes in real time. Take advantage of this capability.

3. *Explore and test channels that might provide better returns.* Set aside a percentage of your budget for experimentation and track progress. You might hit upon a few channels that allow you to change the game. Proven channels are also where your competitors will be, making it more difficult to differentiate.
4. *Set marketing communication goals by channels.* Keep assessing how the channels have performed and determine whether or not you need to make any revisions.

TOUCHPOINTS ROI TRACKER

There are a number of tools that can steer the business planning process where the challenge is to measure impact across the marketing communications mix. One that ZenithOptimedia uses globally is its proprietary Touchpoints ROI Tracker. It steers communications channel planning and to date has involved over 150,000 interviews covering over 2,000 brands in 23 countries.

It enables the marketing effect for a brand to be measured and planned across touchpoints, as well as allowing for a comparison of different strategies against competitors in that brand's sector. Touchpoints ROI Tracker identifies and quantifies the value of every consumer point of contact for a category and its brands, examining the role of each contact point in building brand preference and purchase intent. All forms of consumer contact are measured, including point of sale, point of consumption, one-to-one, word of mouth, sponsorship and mass media.

It is a holistic tool that measures and plans the business effect of all consumer communication and, in so doing, supports the process of managing a marketing communication portfolio.

The Touchpoints ROI Tracker works on the premise that marketing communication's influence on a brand's market share comes from consumer experience of the brand relative to competing brands at each point of contact. Each contact contributes to overall experience of the brand in each category. The Tracker enables a marketer to take money out of a low-performing channel and transfer it into one that is performing better by offering analysis on the ROI of each and every element in the campaign. It therefore allows marketers to handle their communications holistically.

The Tracker adopts the Market Contact Audit©– system, a consumer research-based methodology, developed by consultancy firm

Integration to deliver a variety of ROI diagnostics for each brand in a category. Touchpoints identifies the most cost-effective allocation of marketing budgets from an ROI perspective.

This methodology has five distinct advantages:

1. It allows marketers to shape differentiating strategies from their marketing communications portfolio (see Chapter 8).
2. It identifies and evaluates any consumer point of contact.
3. It assesses the role of contact points along the stages of the path to purchase.
4. It measures and compares the efficiency and the effectiveness of contact points.
5. It unifies communications teams and lists priority actions to improve effectiveness.

Scott Berg, Worldwide Media Director at Hewlett-Packard, enthuses: 'Touchpoints is a valuable process and research tool for measuring and planning improvement in marketing return on investment across all customer contacts. We believe the alignment of brand experience share with market share to be a useful predictor of business outcome from growth in brand experience share.'

Case study: Nescafé – Going beyond traditional media

In 2005, Nescafé in Germany was planning to embark on print and TV activity to promote its new Cappuccino and Latte Macchiato products. In addition to these channels, Touchpoints recommended the inclusion of a major sampling programme as part of their communications portfolio. This would drive trials and sales, as well as word of mouth.

ZenithOptimedia recommended magazine cover sampling, and two publishers agreed to feature the product on the front and back covers of women's titles, as well as include a sample. The ROI was impressive: sales for the total category increased by 3 per cent, while Cappuccino sales were boosted by 22 per cent.

But it was the Latte Macchiato that stole the show – sales increased by 134 per cent. Based on the success of this campaign, Nestlé planned more sampling activity.

A CENTRAL ORGANIZING COMMUNICATION IDEA

Communications can often risk competing for consumers' attention rather than working collaboratively to attract it. When this happens, the impact of the budget is diluted. If you can leverage synergies via a central organizing idea that integrates all the communication, your marketing budget will work harder. Based on consumer insight – not the slogan or the ad line – this articulates what you are trying to communicate. For instance, when O2 was promoting free texts between 6 pm and 8 pm, its central organizing communication idea was 'Happy Hour'. The communication channels ranged from television ads to London taxis giving free rides between 6 pm and 8 pm to deliver a consistent campaign idea.

It's important to maintain the strategic consistency of a big idea rather than independent brand messages. It's a waste of time to put out a plethora of product information dispersed across different platforms, because consumers just don't have the time to decipher each and every brand message they hear, see or read.

Such an exercise is output- rather than outcome-focused. Smart, outcome-led marketing portfolio managers understand that the more the brand's position is strategically integrated into all the brand messages, the more consistent and distinct the company's identity and reputation become. By the same token, the more a big idea is emphasized, the more likely it is that all the marketing communication efforts will have integrity. But if one piece of communication is at odds with another, it can actually undo some of the good results that have been achieved.

O2 goes to get great lengths to ensure that it doesn't over-complicate its communications. 'We offer one single message so that different offers don't compete for customers' attention across all the different touchpoints', says Susie Moore.

This marks out O2 in the cluttered mobile operator space where there's a constant supply of offers and promotions. Consumers respond well to the simplicity of O2's integrated approach: in the past, it has significantly outperformed larger competitors such as Vodafone and Orange with just two-thirds of the budget.

DETERMINING THE CHANNEL MIX BROADLY BASED ON ROI MEASURES

Reliable data help to determine a particular channel mix, and here market-mix modelling, econometric testing and past campaign analysis can assist. You can also choose to use regional media testing to assess how new channels are likely to perform.

Ingrid Murray, Managing Director of Ninah Consulting, comments:

> Metrics are only a means for the people at the top of your company to underline what is important, and to help you to meet their needs. Everything that you do derives from them – and they change according to what you are trying to achieve. One year, management may want to focus on customer acquisition. The next year could be all about creating lifetime value.

One of Ninah's main tools, Investment to Profit Modelling, enables marketers to build sales response curves for each medium used in a particular campaign. The tool can build the cost of reach against the impact of reach, and can then translate that into sales. The response curves can then be linked into profit and loss sheets, allowing marketers to access an ROI figure. Murray says: 'This allows marketers to see how their budgets should be strategically allocated, not just across media, but also across countries and brands.'

LEVERAGING SYNERGIES: DEVELOPMENT

> Integration has become synonymous with matching luggage – the kind of campaign that takes the television ad and turns it into a poster, a direct mail pack and a couple of banner ads… It's not to say that matching luggage is inherently bad. Indeed, consistency in tone and feel is often a vital part of an integrated campaign. But when crudely lifting key visuals from one media to another fails to elicit a response, should anyone be surprised?
>
> Fiona Scott, Managing Director,
> Craik Jones Watson Mitchell Voelkel (Scott 2006)

To avoid the 'matching luggage' syndrome, marketing staff need to assemble and brief their marketing communication partners and align different channel briefs and outcomes. At this stage – even before any winning consumer insights or creative work has been mentioned – metrics need to be determined. The collaborative team needs to agree on how success across the different platforms will be evaluated, as well as on how the metrics will contribute to the strategic goals.

Consumer insight must steer the creative process, and here is where segmentation can work hand in hand with integration. Once the audience has been identified, it not only becomes easier to launch the creative process but it also helps to select the right platform. Media selection is a case of identifying the right tool for the job. The earlier this can be done, the better the chances of boosting your return on communications.

One of Craik Jones Watson Mitchell Voelkel's clients, Gordon's gin, is an example of segmentation and integration in action. It uses advertising to attract younger customers but direct marketing to retain older gin drinkers. Yet each execution, to borrow from the advertising's own tagline, is 'unmistakably Gordon's'.

The consistency, tone and feel of a campaign are crucial because they are the long-term characteristics of each piece of communication. The work needs to match up without each ad having to look exactly the same in each platform, which is where the 'matching luggage' alarm bells should start ringing.

Investing in integration is about deciding where to put your money but also about having a consistent expression of a brand's visual identity – think back to the O2 example. This is increasingly important in a cluttered media environment where attention is limited. The final links in the chain are creativity, strategic thought and consumer insight.

LEVERAGING SYNERGIES: EXECUTION

A marketing investor needs to deploy a broadening portfolio of marketing communications channels not only to reach consumers, but also to influence them at different levels. Prioritizing the allocation of the budget has become a more important issue for driving ROI and should lead the development of the creative messaging.

Creative synergy is important to making communication more productive. There are three different approaches for holistic communications:

1. *Link the theme.* A different brief is required for each part of the campaign, but all briefs are led by the overall campaign brief. For

example, Honda's Dream Factory is led by its agency Wieden+Kennedy London. Other agencies work to individual briefs, but all feed into Honda's proposition, 'The Power of Dreams'.

2. *Link the visuals*. The art direction for the campaign should apply to everything. Examples include the O2 bubbles and British Airways white-type-on-blue house style.

3. *Link the disciplines to a big idea*. Platforms can be autonomous but should link back to an overarching concept. For example, McDonald's 'I'm lovin' it' was a brand repositioning that appeared across all communication, from in-store to online.

A FINAL THOUGHT...

A common misconception is that integration is about making everything look the same. It's not – therein lies the 'matching luggage' treatment. Think instead about driving more effective and productive communication: it is only worthwhile if it is 'felt' by the consumer.

When that happens, integration becomes a value creator rather than a buzzword.

8

Differentiate any way you can

If marketing and sales departments aren't helping to deliver a premium, what are they doing?

Woody Harford, BA's Senior Vice President Commercial, North America

Investors frequently make the same mistakes as marketers in terms of following the herd: they rush to buy stock in companies that are the flavour of the moment rather than analysing whether their purchase is a good long-term investment.

If a company has taken the trouble to differentiate, however, it's a good bet for an investor because it will be more attractive to customers. Differentiation offers the additional advantage of helping marketing communications to stand out, making the marketing investor's job much more straightforward.

One of the most famous examples of a company that zigged when others zagged is Apple. In 1984, when Apple launched its 'Think Different' slogan with its legendary Super Bowl spot, it sold a corporate vision that was anti-establishment. From that point onwards, Apple Macs were for the cool crowd and PCs were for nerds.

In 1998, Apple launched the iMac, a more acceptable item of furniture to have in the front room than a boring beige box. The slogan? 'I think, therefore iMac.' Three years later, the iPod arrived and was trumpeted by a multicoloured integrated campaign that achieved instant stand-out.

Of course, the success of all three Mac products has had as much to do with their aesthetically pleasing design as with the advertising that wraps them up and presents them to consumers; there were other MP3 players on the market before the iPod, and lots of choice in the PC market before the Mac. But by following its own advice to 'Think Different' right from the start, Apple has marked out its territory. It's different to the competition in design, packaging and marketing. Apple has seeped into the national consciousness so much that, like Hoover before it, the iPod has become the generic term for an MP3 player. Thinking differently has paid off for Apple: its shares nearly quadrupled in value in 2004 when iPods started to fly off the shelves.

'Think Different' should be the slogan of all marketers who want their marketing communications to deliver a return. There is no point in being identical to the competition and saying the same thing – only perhaps a bit louder and across more platforms. As Jason Frost, Managing Director of Publicis Blueprint, points out: 'Any successful brand has found a way of differentiating, whether it's through accident or design.'

And each and every sector has its own cliché when it comes to marketing. For cars, it's a series of body shots interspersed with scenic views; hence the praise that was heaped upon Honda's 'Cog'. The ad, by Wieden+Kennedy in 2003, showed how a Honda Accord was constructed by filming a complex chain reaction involving 85 individual vehicle parts. Subsequent W+K ads maintained the Honda hallmark of being somehow *different* to other car brands, with 'Grrr' using animation to promote Honda's cleaner diesel engine, and 'Choir', a spot for its Civic model, which featured a 60-strong choir imitating the sounds by the car. The ads buck the trend in the car sector because they don't just show the product.

For beers, humour is de rigueur, so Stella Artois, with its arty, cinematic communications, is memorable. For banks, an erstwhile seriousness dominates, giving Halifax in the UK (see Chapter 12) instant appeal when it took a more light-hearted approach.

Differentiation can come from product benefits or clever communication. When Unilever's Elida Gibbs division launched its mild shampoo brand, Timotei, in the early 1980s, there was little about the product that was radically different to what was already available. Yet because women were showering daily and starting to wash their hair more frequently, the shampoo identified and occupied a new gap in the market for a mild shampoo that was ideal for frequent hair-washing. Sales soared.

As Pamela Robertson (1998) points out, 'The real brilliance was in the targeting and positioning of Timotei... By positioning Timotei as a natural herbal shampoo with the attendant visual cues, the implication of gentleness was implicit. The differentiation was much more in the positioning than in a major product breakthrough.'

The ideal situation for marketers is if they are promoting a product that already offers consumers a real unique benefit rather than a perceived one.

Case study: General Electric – Using Ecomagination

In 2003, General Electric (GE) launched a new slogan – Imagination at Work – which topped a poll of US consumers through an online vote hosted by Yahoo! Two years later, it launched a business strategy, Ecomagination, which formed the basis of a subsequent marketing campaign. This achieved genuine stand-out thanks to highlighting the unique nature of GE's product portfolio and environmentally friendly stance.

The global initiative, which launched in May 2005, has four goals: doubling the R&D investment by 2010, introducing a more extensive portfolio of energy-efficient products, reducing greenhouse gas emissions by 2012, and keeping the public up to date about GE's progress.

GE wanted to address its customers' needs and this meant helping them to reduce carbon emissions, make cost efficiencies and be mindful of their impact on the environment. The wind turbines and eco-locomotives featured in the communication – which ran across print, online, TV and outdoor – sold out, and GE's revenues increased from $6.2 billion in 2004 to $10 billion in 2005. The business objective is to reach $20 billion by 2010. GE came top in *Fortune*'s 'Most Admired Companies' list in 2006.

VALUE VERSUS PRICE

Decreasing price to increase a brand's fortunes is a dangerous drug. While its effects are often dramatic and instantaneous, its repercussions are insidious and long-standing. Businesses that chase volume by cutting price invariably end up sacrificing value, sometimes in the short term and almost always in the long run... The City intuitively understands this cycle, tending to mark down stock the moment price heads south.

Richard Storey, Planning Director, M&C Saatchi (Storey, 2005)

The biggest advantage of differentiating your product is that brands don't get sucked into competing on the lowest common denominator: price. Marketing is the most important vehicle through which you can maintain or grow product or service margins.

A combination of low cost and high quality will always be a hit with consumers. In Europe and the United States, over 50 per cent of the population shops at mass merchants such as Wal-Mart, buys flights from low-cost operators and visits websites for bargains. Value players attract customers with low prices and 'good-enough' quality, and this can serve as a differentiator in its own right. But when too many companies occupy this space, they fail to be distinctive to consumers.

Rishad Tobaccowala, the chief executive of the consultancy Denuo, also points out that competing on price has serious ramifications for products and services with competitors in China and India, where manufacturing and servicing costs are a fraction of the price of Europe and the United States. He observes: 'Marketing officers tend to spend too much on the cost line rather than on the revenue or imagination line.'

Target, the US department store chain, is one retailer that eschewed the bargain basement approach for a strategy that set it apart from the competition. Founded in 1962, its market niche was described in the 1980s as 'upscale discount'. Designers like Michael Graves started to produce goods for the store. In a nod to its own delusions of grandeur, its advertising slogan became 'C'est Target' (with Target pronounced with a French accent, 'tar-jay'). Continuing its upscale ascent, a recent media first for the brand was to take every ad in the *New Yorker*. Sales continue on an upward curve, and Target opened 60 new stores across the United States in 2005 as its 'design for all' proposition resonated with the country's middle class.

If Target had followed a similar tactic to Wal-Mart or Kmart – two stores that pride themselves on offering consumers rock-bottom prices – it would have been lost in the wilderness. By differentiating itself from the start and positioning its range as more premium, it created a space into which it could grow.

Case study: Westin – The heavenly hotel

The Westin Hotel invested in beds that had double the number of springs and that were smoother and softer than average hotel beds. Westin organized its marketing around the 'Heavenly bed' and has since added to the 'Heavenly' range with a two-nozzled shower, soap, shampoo and towels.

A week after the bed's introduction in 1999, Westin guests were enquiring about how they could purchase it for their own homes. More than 30,000 guests have now bought a Heavenly bed.

A Westin survey showed increases in guest loyalty and satisfaction, and it was surely no coincidence that 'comfort of bed' scored 8.96 out of 10 in 1999, a figure that rose to 9.19 in 2004. Home orders are still popular, with the Heavenly line predicted to generate $8 million in annual revenues.

HOW TO DIFFERENTIATE YOUR BRAND

> There is no reason for consumers to change their brand if a new product is a copy of what they are currently buying... Products need to be different either in reality or perceptually. The former is preferable but not always achievable. But perception can be just as persuasive.
>
> Pamela Robertson (1998)

There are several ways in which products can stand out, and they can be linked to other aspects of business, such as a distribution strategy or promotional variables. When it comes to marketing, however, there are a number of tactics you can use to create a point of difference for your product.

This list of 10 is by no means intended to be exhaustive, but rather to offer some examples of routes to markets, and products or services that have successfully adopted them.

Each one is designed to follow the golden rule of differentiation: *give the customer a specific benefit in return for buying your product.* This benefit should offer value rather than rely on price as a differentiating feature:

1. *Emphasize a positive aspect of business practice.* Consumers are becoming more ethically conscious and want information about

how products are made. Reports of sweatshop labour continue to haunt big global businesses such as The Gap, Sears and Nike, with some consumers boycotting their product lines altogether. Other brands are using their credentials in this area as a selling point. American Apparel claims that its business is 'sweatshop-free'; the company manufactures its range of cotton basics in Los Angeles.

Sustainability has also been a big differentiator for some brands, with certain products using their progress in this area as a selling point. The UK retailer Marks & Spencer has made its business more sustainable in that it sells only Fairtrade tea and coffee and has invested in a sustainable fishing supply chain. It also produces more environmentally friendly clothes that need less dry cleaning and don't use harsh dyes. The 'look behind the label' campaign spoke directly to consumers, informing them about these changes, and appealed to the retail chain's upmarket, ethically conscious customers. Soon after the campaign launched, Marks & Spencer's share price bucked the trend in a depressed retail environment.

2. *Use humour.* You don't normally associate ads for laxatives with a sense of humour, but French agency Jean et Montmarin's 2002 TV spot for Ducolax was different. It starts with a woman packing her suitcase surrounded by her family, and a sense of sadness hangs heavy in the air. But she doesn't leave the house as we expect her to do; instead she heads for the toilet. Thanks to Ducolax, constipation sufferers no longer need to spend hours – or, as the suitcase suggests, days – locked in their bathrooms. What makes this ad even more brave is the fact that ads for medication are strictly regulated in France, making one with a light-hearted approach even more memorable.

3. *Take the simple route.* Never underestimate the value of simplifying a message for consumers. There is an unbelievable amount of clutter in all media, and consumers don't have the time to figure out what each and every message is trying to communicate. O2 has benefited from cutting through the clutter in mobile communications and by being crystal clear about its product benefits by focusing on just one message at a time. This means that consumers on different tariffs are receiving the same message about the company. The consistent visual identity also contributes towards a brand 'voice', which some of O2's competitors lack.

4. *Leverage national heritage.* When consumers can see where a brand comes from, it is easier for them to tap into what it is that's on offer. Sweden, for instance, brings to mind relaxation, clean design and simplicity. So it's no surprise that Ikea uses Swedish names for its

products and further underlines its provenance in-store by selling national dishes in its café. Despite using localized advertising to appeal to different attitudes towards furniture and domestic life in the countries where it operates, it is unmistakably Swedish, most prominently through its love of blue and yellow, the colours of the country's flag.

5. *Build trust.* If consumers feel that a product is tried and trusted, they are more likely to use it rather than to re-evaluate their brand choice. British Airways, for instance, consistently tops the 'most trusted' box in the airlines category in the Reader's Digest Trusted Brands survey. While consumers may have initially flocked to low-cost airlines, when the plane doesn't leave on time or lands miles out of a city centre, consumers want to return to a name they can trust instead. Similarly, the CEO of Tesco, Terry Leahy (2005: 40) made the point that: 'Trust will matter more and more. As the world shrinks but people's lives become more complicated, people will turn to brands and products they know and trust. Perceptions of trust will be shaped not just by price or service, but also by issues like the environment, health, labour conditions and animal welfare.'

6. *Understand and empathize.* If you make an effort to be on the same wavelength as your target market you will stand a good chance of striking a chord with them and being front of mind. Radio and TV ads for the recruitment site Monster by Saatchi & Saatchi follow the theme of 'inner voices' where unhappy employees are taunted by voices compounding their situation and are encouraged to visit the recruitment site. Timing also plays a crucial factor – in January 2004, Monster played on the despondency that many workers feel returning to work after a break for the holidays. The campaign implores: 'Beware of the voices.'

7. *Don't underestimate reliability.* On the face of it, reliability seems like a dull product characteristic with limited attraction for consumers. On the other hand, for certain products it's a must. Who wants a car that is anything other than reliable? Toyota has managed to create a stand-out in Europe by combining the fact that its cars are reliable with gentle humour positioning them as objects of desire.

8. *Use a celebrity.* Celebrities tend to be used to advertise lifestyle products such as cars, mobile phone brands, designer clothes, perfumes and aftershaves. There aren't many that would happily promote crisps. This makes former England football captain Gary Lineker's 11-year stint as the face of Walkers crisps a differentiator. There's not only a long-term relationship between Lineker and the

brand, but there's also differentiation in the ads themselves, with Lineker dressing up in a variety of roles, including a housewife and Austin Powers. The Lineker/Walkers association is in stark contrast to the use of English footballer David Beckham, who has been the face of Police sunglasses, Vodafone, Pepsi and Motorola.

9. *Use consumers.* Pepsi was one of the first brands to do this with its Pepsi Taste Challenge, followed by the Pepsi Generation. Today, more brands are inviting consumers to help differentiate their product, either by being the face of the brand or by helping to generate communications content. Dove's 'real beauty' campaign uses real people rather than models and has used that as a spring-board into debate around our different ideas of what beauty means. The Dove campaign stood out because it was different to the norm for its sector: there were no airbrushed models with alabaster skin.

10. *Associate.* Mobile phone operator Orange has associated itself with film when so many of its competitors are trying to 'own' music. Orange not only offers two-for-one cinema tickets through its Orange Wednesdays initiative, but it also runs film-making competitions and runs tongue-in-cheek cinema ads featuring the 'Orange Film Academy' that remind film-goers to turn off their phones during the movie. It celebrates up-and-coming acting talent with its Rising Star award and makes film recommendations on its website.

The I word

When trying to differentiate your product, there will be numerous references to the I word: insight. This is a much-used word in marketing communications and is responsible for reports produced by market research companies or planners trying to get to the bottom of a brand, where it fits in the marketplace and who it is trying to target.

As with marketing communications, the focus needs to be on the outcome rather than the output, so findings should be summarized into bullet points. Mark Sherrington, the author of *Added Value* (2003: 49), suggests asking five questions that challenge the strength of the insight, or what he terms 'how to spot the eureka moment':

1. Is it fresh? Do you feel that you are looking at your market and your mission in a new way, even if the insight is really simple?
2. Is it discerning? Do you feel you can compare it with other viable alternatives and confidently say it is better?

3. Is it penetrating? Does it get beyond superficial analysis and conventional wisdom? Do you feel you have gone deeper into the market than anyone else before you?
4. Is it the product or the fusion of more than one insight or, if you have chosen one simple insight, can you see how it links to other insights?
5. Does it inspire you and others? Are the implications already starting to flow for how you can change strategy, innovate, communicate in new ways and see different things you will now measure for success?

Case study: Mandarin Oriental Hotel Group – Differentiating the brand

Challenge

When M&C Saatchi Hong Kong started to work on the Mandarin Oriental business, it realized that there was no clear leader in the luxury hotel sector, despite Mandarin Oriental having the quality of customer experience to secure that positioning. What's more, hotel advertising tended to be bland and product-led, whereas Mandarin Oriental wanted to put the customer at the heart of the message. Finally, Mandarin Oriental needed to act like a luxury brand rather than a luxury hotel group.

Solution

Conventional advertising was shunned. There were to be no shots of the hotel, no ads promoting individual hotels and no reservation details. Instead, M&C Saatchi wanted to reflect the affinity that Mandarin Oriental guests have with the brand.

M&C Saatchi's solution was to leverage the group's iconic logo to make a link with the celebrities featured in the ads using three simple words: 'He's/She's a fan.' The personalities in the ads – which have included Barry Humphries, Jane Seymour and Jerry Hall – were rewarded with a $10,000 donation to a charity.

Crucially, the group's new chief executive, Edouard Ettedgui, had ambitious plans to expand the Asia-based hotel chain across Europe and the United States. The 'fan' campaign matched his vision for the brand.

Results

In 2003, research conducted by the *New Yorker* magazine in the form of the Starch Readership Survey evaluated all the ads that ran in the publication the previous autumn. Even on a comparatively small media spend, Mandarin Oriental came top in recall against other long-standing and high-spending advertisers such as American Express. The ad also ranked first in terms of brand attribution. The campaign has redefined its category and created a sought-after global brand.

AVOID COMMODITIZATION

If you fall into the trap of safe, expected marketing choices, you will only add to the commoditization of your product or service. If you can think of examples of 'safe' marketing, you clearly possess an amazing memory; one characteristic of such communications is that they are instantly forgettable.

Whether or not marketers have segmented, integrated, implemented methods of tracking the success of particular channels or maximized their customer equity is irrelevant if a piece of communication remains ignored.

The biggest cost any marketer faces is not being noticed.

There are different tactics that offer marketing communications portfolio managers a way of avoiding being ignored. Below, we have picked the most prominent and cherry-picked examples from around the world. All of them prove how getting noticed is all about looking at the bigger picture rather than the next advertising campaign.

The name game

A company's name has to work beyond marketing, so it's essential to invest in one that is appropriate, memorable and distinctive, particularly now that search advertising is on the increase. The dotcom boom and bust in the late 1990s showed that companies that don't have the advantage of a memorable name are dead in the water from the start.

Perhaps the best example comes from one of the dullest sectors imaginable: directory enquiries services. In the UK, the telecom watchdog Oftel switched off the '192' directory enquiries number in 2002 to break the monopoly by the national telecom, BT. Numbers beginning '118' were randomly assigned to directory services operators.

The US directory company InfoNXX owned The Number, one of the new players. The Number invested £2 million of its advertising budget on acquiring the most memorable number – 118 118 – from a competitor.

It proved to be a shrewd investment. While all the numbers began with '118', many were obscure combinations. Some of the services had problems in differentiating themselves because their number was tricky to remember in the first place and didn't lend itself to a strong creative idea.

With 118 118, The Number was able to launch an integrated campaign, spearheaded by its ad agency WCRS, starring two runners with the number '118'. The runners were everywhere throughout 2003 and their catchphrase – Got Your Number – entered the vernacular.

It also got ahead on the competition by launching early – long before the number went live – so it was already front of mind before communications for other '118' numbers began to appear.

By 2004, The Number had built up a 44 per cent market share. BT, the national telecom that used to own the directory services market, had just 34 per cent. The return on investment is compelling: on an investment of £13.5 million, the campaign's return was £45.4 million. The strong marketing communications strategy could not have emerged without the easiest number to remember – the name proved to be a critical first investment and proves the impact that such a decision can have on the entire communication portfolio.

Media magic

Marketers maximize their chances of being noticed if they hit on either a product or a communications benefit that will appeal to consumers and then they differentiate in their selection of media too. The *Economist* campaign was different for using posters rather than global TV channels such as CNN and CNBC, backed up by press work. The differentiation is as much about being faithful to the outdoor medium as the strong creative.

One of our Marketing ROI stars, British Airways, had the novel media idea of 'turning New York blue' to make it stand out from the crowd.

BA's distinctive blue colour was found adorning bizarre properties such as deli bags and apartment construction sites. By using British words – 'takeaway' on the deli bags and 'flats' on the building sites – it surrounded New Yorkers with authentic 'Britishness' at every turn of their day by extending the media idea beyond traditional touchpoints to give it much more impact.

Increasingly, marketers are realizing that an appropriate medium can enhance a creative treatment and bring it to life. In Japan, two examples embody this idea: Northwest Airlines used the inside panel of office window cleaners' external boxes to target a business audience, while Knorr Cup A Soup communicated warmth by writing the brand name in simulated steam on the windows of commuter trains.

Similarly, in Shanghai, Y Plus Yoga Centre wanted to promote its school on a negligible budget. Leo Burnett showed the flexibility of a yoga practitioner on the bendy stems of drinking straws and placed them at the juice bars frequented by the health-conscious target audience. Posters followed that fixed to the wall only halfway up, so that the top half of the poster would fall over, giving the illusion of the yoga practitioner bending backwards. Attendance at yoga classes improved considerably, and the bendy straws are now collectors' items.

Wrapping paper

If the packaging for a product is distinctive and appealing, it can be one of the most important investments of all in the marketing communication portfolio.

When ING launched in the United States in 2001, its distinctive orange colour helped it to stand out as a financial services brand where the predominant colours tend to be blue and green. And Pepsi-Cola differentiated Pepsi from Coke in the early 1970s by designing plastic bottles that were lighter and more transportable than Coke's glass one. Consumers will buy a product because of seductive packaging too, or even because the store bags are attractive to them in some way. Camper shoes, for instance, have red-and-white bags by the Catalan designer Martí Guixé scrawled with messages like 'If you don't need it, don't buy it'.

In the United States, L'Oréal Fructis shampoo differentiated in its packaging by using distinctive green upside-down bottles that stood out on pharmacy shelves. This echoes the recency theory outlined in Chapter 5, which refers to how purchasing decisions often hinge on the advertising closest to the point of sale. Packaging can work as advertising in itself, and needs to be carefully considered.

Courting controversy

A marketing communications strategy that is controversial doesn't demand a huge media spend in today's world of blogs and links; it can show once or twice and, with the right PR management, will be picked up by bloggers and community sites such as YouTube.com. Coke recently showed its ad with a soundtrack sung by the White Stripes frontman Jack White just once on TV in the UK. Yet because controversy raged over whether or not White had 'sold out' for penning the track 'Love Is the Truth' specifically for the ad, the ad was picked up by news sources and blogs and took on a life of its own.

Sparking debate

The traditional way that marketers spoke to consumers was by informing them that their products and services were the best available because they offered certain benefits and qualities that the competition couldn't quite match. As that tactic has become hackneyed, more innovative ways have emerged for marketers to grab attention, not least to persuade consumers to think a little more deeply about issues that go beyond simple purchasing behaviour. In other words, advertising used to sell dreams; today it's more interested in stirring up debate.

The Unilever brand Dove found this when it launched its Campaign for Real Beauty. Dove differentiated by inviting both women and men rather than the media and advertising to define beauty. Instead of starring the usual glossy, stick-thin, airbrushed models, billboards and ads featured real women – flaws and all. The global campaign launched in Europe in 2004 and asked 'Grey or gorgeous?', 'Wrinkled or wonderful?', 'Ugly spots or beauty spots?' Dove invited consumers to join in a debate about what constitutes beauty. Throughout 2005, the campaign rolled out across the United States and Asia, and sales of Dove products increased by 163 per cent. Unilever's research arm, Economatrician, claimed that Dove was 2005's most talked-about ad campaign. The brand has also set up its self-esteem fund to help women with body-image issues.

AOL encouraged debate over whether the internet is a good or bad thing through its 'discuss' site, while a long-copy cross-track poster campaign for Orange weighed up mobile phones. Both brands accepted that not every single consumer was cock-a-hoop about new technology, admitting that in fact the enabling qualities of these new media were not always a good thing. HSBC's global 'point of view' campaign broadens out this proposition by using simple posters to direct people online to debate subjects such as the viability of wind energy.

Debates don't always have to be a serious business, and some brands have used the fact that they divide opinion to have fun. The yeast extract spread Marmite became a much-loved national brand once again in the UK just by being honest about how people feel about the product through its 'You either love it or you hate it' strategy. Ads that showed a man gagging after kissing a girl who's just taken a bite from a Marmite-smeared bagel encapsulated the idea, and Marmite translated the strategy into other platforms, such as online where it has a 'love' site and a 'hate' site. In 2002, Marmite enjoyed a sales uplift of £47 million following an investment of £12 million.

Using spoofs

Spoofs have become a particularly popular way to differentiate for marketing investors because they have the bonus effect of generating PR and thus more attention for the brand. Consumers are also more likely to remember spoofs.

In the United States, Crispin Porter + Bogusky invented the 'counterfeit Mini' campaign – where 'fake' cars were passed off as Minis. It generated extra attention when ads for the deliberately ridiculous-looking vehicles were placed in the classified ad pages of motoring press titles like *Auto Trader*. Meanwhile, public information leaflets pleaded: 'Protect yourself from the humiliation of owning a fake!'

DDB Paris produced an integrated campaign for SNCF Voyages – the flight-booking division of the national railways, SNCF, which suggested that a sub-Atlantic train service would connect Paris to New York in just eight hours. Radio stations and blogs picked up on the outdoor and online ads. The unorthodox activity promoted SNCF's flight-booking service – Voyages-sncf.com (VSF) – to encourage potential customers to realize that it offers much more than train tickets. After just one week, over 1 million people had visited the website and over 80 per cent of people interviewed by Ipsos understood that VSF offered a myriad of travel services.

Amnesty International's 'protect the human' campaign featured a cinema ad by Mother London starring Teleshop, a spoof shopping channel selling guns and weapons. Other elements in the campaign included a fake roadshow that showed the ease with which an AK47 can be assembled. The incongruous environment was to hammer home the point that one person every minute dies as a result of armed violence.

Emotion

Charities and non-profit organizations tend to play heavily on emotion in their marketing communications, but other brands use it to their advantage too. Crown Paints was one of them. At the end of the 1990s in the UK, Crown Paints was losing out to Dulux and own-branded paint products. So it brought colour into its communication, allowing Crown to occupy the emotional high ground. To differentiate its Breatheasy virtually odour-free paint, the Crown ad showed smartly dressed people who had unwittingly leaned against a freshly painted wall. By 2000, the Crown brand had grown by almost 66 per cent.

WHEN NOT TO DIFFERENTIATE...

According to Michael Porter, the professor at Harvard Business School, there are three strategies open to businesses: low price, technology or differentiation, depending on where they are positioned in the market-place. While marketing communications must be used if a differentiation strategy is being pursued, it's also important for firms that are seeking to undercut the competition and that are keen to encourage consumers to switch to their lower-priced alternative: they will show the similarity between the products available and focus on how their pricing is more competitive. Supermarkets use this trick on everyday branded products to boost footfall in their outlets.

EDITING CONSUMER CHOICE

Differentiation helps choices to be made, purchases to be bought and paid for, and habits to form. Without it, consumers wouldn't be able to articulate their preferences. As *The Paradox of Choice: Why more is less* (Schwartz, 2005: 42) says: 'Everything in life is choice. Every second of every day we are choosing and there are always alternatives. Human existence is defined by the choices people make.'

And the choices made by marketing portfolio managers must mark out their products and services if they are to stand a chance of being noticed by consumers.

Smart investors think different.

9

Engagement and experience are the new 30-second ads

> When I was at design school, people would ask: 'Who do you follow, the Stones or the Beatles?' In a similar sense, people follow brands. You don't persuade people to follow you by saying: 'I want to be your friend.' But when someone is interesting, you're drawn to them. Marketing is much the same.
>
> John Hegarty, Worldwide Creative Director, Bartle Bogle Hegarty

Think about the 'I' in ROI. So much emphasis is placed on the 'R' – or the return – that the investment angle can be overlooked. Yet strong, original and creative communication ideas should be regarded by marketing investors as a vital element in their portfolio.

A strong creative idea chimes with the target market and will stick around, regardless of how the communications strategy evolves. For instance, who doesn't know that BA is 'the world's favourite airline' or that Avis tries harder? Who doesn't link 'Whassup?' with Budweiser, 'I'm lovin' it' with McDonald's or Fairy liquid with soft hands? And it's common knowledge around the globe that Olay helps combat the signs of ageing and that Guinness is worth waiting for.

Whereas many of those associations were built with the help of TV, the rules have changed in the new economy. Without engaging customers, seizing their attention and offering them an experience, products stand little chance of being noticed. This means that all the efforts that marketers may have made in setting up the right metrics, segmenting their audience and managing their communication port-folio could end up delivering disappointing returns. This is why the 'I' in ROI is just as important as the 'R': investing in appropriate and imag-inative creative work minimizes the risk of disappointing returns.

Our Marketing ROI stars exemplify an ability to engage consumers and have the ROI figures to prove it. O2, for instance, on a much tighter budget than its rivals, not only built a brand that resonated with its customers, but also staged events such as the O2 Wireless Festival in Hyde Park. Toyota created buzz around the Aygo launch with music tie-ins and events – a strategy that saw it outperform competitors by selling more cars at under a quarter of the average marketing cost per unit. Meanwhile, Toyota's Lexus marque got in front of its upmarket target audience and encouraged them to sign up for test drives by being where they were: in airports and at hotels at Europe's elite holiday spots.

P&G is expert in engagement, whether it's an online 'big sister' hub for teenage girls, www.beinggirl.com to promote its femcare brands, a *Marie Claire* cover that used sound-chip technology to reproduce orgasmic cries from its TV ads for Herbal Essences, or downloadable music tracks on the Tide washing powder site, www.tide.com.

And British Airways has moved with the times, finding new ways to engage with its audience. In an age where low-cost carriers were rising to prominence by stripping back flights to provide a value expe-rience, BA tapped into what its customers liked about flying and offered in-flight food and freebies for kids. In its marketing too, it found new ways to engage with consumers. On the Heathrow Express train, for instance, it used actors to talk about the convenience of online check-in at www.ba.com. This echoed an idea that BA used in 1992, when an interactive cinema ad showing a couple enjoying a romantic break in Paris – thanks to BA's competitive prices – incurred the wrath of a female member of the audience. This person, an actor planted in the audience, heckles the screen because the man in Paris is her boyfriend. The two-timing boyfriend attempts to explain but winds up being dumped by both women.

In the USA, BA attached itself to the TV show *Queer Eye for the Straight Guy,* and renamed it *Queer Eye for the British Guy* for two London episodes that featured BA first-class cabins and flat beds. It also backed a 'bands reunited' series on VH1 where it helped to reunite 1980s British bands such as Haircut 100 and ABC. This sponsorship – which used TV, online, print, radio, in-store, airport signage and in-flight entertainment

– was intended to engage with younger, affluent travellers with the means to pay for business-class flights to London.

Advertisers like British Airways that boast an impressive heritage of TV advertising have increasingly been looking beyond the 30-second spot. While there's no doubt that the doom-mongers are sounding the death knell for this unit of advertising, TV spots can still perform well in ROI terms as a key element of many marketing investment portfolios, and there's also no denying that consumers appreciate clever, outcome-based communication. For instance, over 100 UK consumers wrote to Stella Artois requesting copies of print ads where sequences from famous movies were embedded into everyday British life. The ads promoted Stella's 'classic films' series where the beer brand underlines its link with cinema by hosting screenings in locations that are relevant to the film – in 2005, for example, it showed *Birdman of Alcatraz* on Alcatraz Island. It's no coincidence that, since it started advertising 15 years ago, Stella has led the UK's £6.5 billion UK premium lager market. Today it is the UK's third-largest grocery brand.

As the Stella example shows, if compelling creative ideas offer appropriate means of engagement consumers' propensity to purchase will increase because they have a clear idea of what a particular brand stands for. Marketing communications that can bring products to life and integrate them into the real world as part of a 3-D experience – just like the BA cinema ad from 1992 – are a preferable investment to 2-D ads because they instantly differentiate. As discussed in Chapter 8, any product that manages to differentiate from the start is well placed to deliver more impressive returns on investment.

Offering consumers a particular experience gives them a chance to think about a product or service that they may not have actively considered in the past. It also builds loyalty among existing customers, facilitating customer retention and effectively blotting out the competition. And marketing portfolio managers who invest in capturing the attention of mavens are hitting on a particularly efficient strategy because the mavens will spread the gospel on their behalf.

THE MAGIC OF MAVENS

If a product, experience or service can excite the interest of mavens – either of the professional (critics and specialists) or amateur (bloggers and consumer reviewers) variety – it can expect to enjoy a considerable return on marketing investment. Not only is the brand less likely to have spent millions on traditional mass-media marketing, but the fact that a third party is taking an interest makes it a far more credible proposition in the eyes of cynical consumers weary of the hard sell.

Mavens carry considerable sway in particular sectors, influencing consumers to behave a certain way. Gaming is one such sector. When Microsoft is about to launch a new Xbox console, it will create maximum hype among gaming enthusiast mavens. Teasers offering snippets of information about the new console will be leaked on to particular sites and blogs by mavens, sending clue-hungry fans on a wild goose chase. This was the case when Xbox launched its 360 console in November 2005. A consortium of different agencies worked together on the launch: AKQA and lead Xbox agency McCann Erickson San Francisco were joined by JDK Design and 72andSunny, a Californian boutique. When the website www.origenxbox360.com appeared, fans turned it upside down in a search for clues.

There was no media spend: the campaign relied purely on PR and word of mouth.

INVEST IN INSPIRATION

Communications agencies talk in terms of experience, engagement, interactivity and entertainment. It's no longer enough just to tell consumers that you're out there; you need to excite their imagination and, most importantly of all, inspire them. That way, they're drawn to one particular product as opposed to its being just another one of the bevy of brands all battling for consumers' attention.

John Hegarty states: 'Great brands inspire people to come to them.' He reels off a list of clients that he has worked on since the 1980s at BBH and that he has helped to elevate to this position, including Levi's, Audi and Häagen-Dazs. He reflects: 'When those brands are at their best, they inspire people to come to them. Great brands say "I stand for this" and communicate in a way that captures people's imagination.'

Yet few companies manage to inspire people, according to Hegarty. He says: 'I'm constantly encouraged by the attitude of consumers. What they want is more interesting, exciting and different things. Yet most companies are failing to deliver that in terms of their product, distribution and attitude.'

Smart marketing investors recognize that consumers aren't on tenter-hooks waiting for their next ad to be broadcast on TV. They know that, with so many products competing for their attention, one way they can engage is by respecting their audience, or even by rewarding them.

Olivier Altmann, Chairman of the Publicis Worldwide Creative Board and the Executive Creative Director of Publicis Conseil, suggests: 'Treat your audience like your best friend, your child or your wife, and don't treat consumers like they're stupid. That's the first rule of the communication process. Advertising is about persuading people to buy something from you, so offer them something to get their attention: a funny joke, a tip or a happy moment.'

EXPERIENCE, NOT POSSESSIONS

The products and services that are attracting fans are the ones that understand that life is busy and time is at a premium. In affluent nations – the world's largest ad markets – there is more emphasis than ever among the middle classes on spending money on experiences as opposed to flashy possessions.

Expensive holidays, the beauty business and gym chains are all booming industries, and pet owners spend extraordinary amounts of money pampering their loved ones – in the UK, the pet market is currently worth £3.8 billion, and this figure is expected to rise to £4.26 billion in 2010.

Tickets for events exchange hands for hundreds of thousands of dollars on eBay. Gigs and festivals sell out seconds after the tickets are available online. People are less defined by what they do for a living, where they come from, where they live or what they own; they're far more likely to be shaped by the experiences that they've had, whether it's living or working overseas, travelling, extreme sports or philanthropy.

Chapter 8 showed how marketing portfolio managers intending to compete on price are likely to get stuck in the slow lane. Instead, if you can offer customers a positive experience of your brand or a means to engage with them, the chances of your marketing investments delivering impressive profits are considerably higher.

Service brands – particularly retailers – are particularly well placed to create experiences for consumers. Indeed, with the rise and rise of e-commerce, it's been a key way for many of them to differentiate. For instance, customers at the Levi's store in San Francisco could shrink-fit their jeans by sinking into a bathtub in a nod to BBH's famous 'launderette' commercial from 1982, while Nokia's website promises a great deal from its flagship store: 'Here's a store quite unlike any other. It's an experience. A chance to get to grips with Nokia. Feel our products, try out our services, and figure out what will fit perfectly... it's all about offering an innovative and inspiring interactive experience.'

The Apple store on Regent Street opened in November 2004 and gave the first 300 customers the chance to spend £249 on a mystery lucky-dip bag, which Apple said would contain kit worth more than £700. Five thousand people showed up. Helen Dickinson, the Head of Retail at KPMG, commented in her *Marketing* column on 24 May 2006: 'Apple recognizes that a presence on high-profile streets in the world's leading cities is vital, and its glitzy stores allow the brand to showcase its products in the best possible environment.'

In this chapter, we champion companies that have invested in pioneering ways of connecting with consumers. They are clear about their proposition and what they stand for. They regularly invest in offering customers some kind of experience or a chance to engage that cannot be matched by competitors. Such investments have led to substantial profits. We focus on Starbucks, Nike, Hewlett-Packard and Axe.

Case study: Starbucks – Creating the coffee experience

Starbucks is a flagship example of a brand that has created a market, engaged with its customers and offered them such an enjoyable experience that they keep coming back for more.

It opened its first outlet in Seattle in 1971, and branched out into takeaway coffee from selling grounds. By February 2006, there were 7,600 Starbucks outlets in the United States and over 3,000 further afield. It continues to be an unstoppable force: Chairman Howard Schultz wants China to be the second-biggest market after the United States; the plan is eventually to operate 15,000 stores in the United States and another 15,000 beyond, increasing both revenue and profit by 20 per cent annually. And if ever a brand exemplified the important relationship between customer retention and ROI, it's Starbucks: regular customers visit Starbucks 18 times a month, making it the world's most frequently visited retailer. Thirty-four million customers around the globe visit a Starbucks every week.

Starbucks hit Europe in 1998, first landing in the UK. In that market alone, it has been a huge hit, defining the sector and spawning a wave of competitors. Allegra Strategies predicts that the coffee chains – which now also include Caffè Nero and Costa Coffee – will grow by 8.9 per cent to be worth £1.4 billion in the UK by 2008.

A Mintel report (2006a) on the UK market estimates that the market has grown by 109 per cent since 1999. There are an estimated 1,604 branded coffee shops in the UK. The growth of the coffee chains has triggered more coffee drinking in the home: total UK coffee sales hit £680 million in 2005, according to Mintel, 15 per cent (£100 million) of which was fresh or ground coffee – a big behavioural shift in a country where, 20 years ago, the height of sophistication for a coffee in the home meant a hastily prepared cup of Nescafé Gold Blend.

Starbucks has not only popularized the coffee experience, but it has attached a high premium to it. Not so long ago, a cup of coffee was served in a white polystyrene cup and cost $1 at the most. Today, it can cost up to five times that amount, and the choice is dizzying to non-aficionados.

Starbucks' revelation – that it is the social encounters that surround coffee that are important rather than the drink itself – has been an immensely profitable one. Analysts agree that, with rising monthly sales that exceed $750 million, Starbucks is outperforming the market, and some even predict that it will overtake McDonald's as the world's largest fast-food brand.

Starbucks is not a big-budget advertiser; its success has come about via its ubiquity. It has firmly established its presence on major high streets, airports and shopping malls in Europe, the United States and Asia by creating a relaxing experience around what was previously a humdrum activity: having a cup of coffee.

Now others are piggybacking Starbucks to reach its affluent crowd of coffee-lovers. The movie *Akeelah and the Bee* was promoted in the United States and Canada via Starbucks outlets, and other film releases may follow. Music has been another brand fit. In 1999, Starbucks bought the chain of US record stores Hear Music for $8 million and, through that acquisition, started to bring music to its customers.

In 2005, 5,000 Starbucks outlets sold CDs – a year-on-year increase of 307 per cent – and the chain exclusively promoted new tracks by Alanis Morissette and Bob Dylan. A Ray Charles compilation, *Genius Loves Company*, which was initiated and co-funded by Starbucks, won six Grammy awards in 2005.

Learning about new music and film releases while relaxing in an armchair with a cappuccino is one pastime; reading is another. Starbucks has partnered Borders and has in-store cafés at many of its outlets. Other coffee chains have followed suit with other book retailers. Explaining the link-up, the Borders website frames the arrangement in characteristic 'experience' language: 'The Starbucks and Borders relationship aims to provide a unique environment that encourages consumers to relax in-store whether it's browsing for books with a coffee or sat in Starbucks with their favourite beverage reviewing their finds.'

Now Starbucks Chairman Howard Schultz has announced his plans to sell books in-store, featuring popular authors in the way that *Akeelah and the Bee* was promoted.

Such link-ups extend Starbucks' product offering so that it has positive cultural associations that appeal to its customer base. As the Euromonitor International UK analyst Samantha Thorburn observed in *Marketing* on 15 March 2006: 'Orders such as a "skinny double-shot decaff high-foam latte to go" have turned the traditional cup of coffee into a lifestyle statement.'

Case study: Nike – Just doing it

Following a surge of popularity throughout the 1990s, Nike began to lose its edge. Once famous for its celebrity-studded ads starring the likes of Michael Jordan, Andre Agassi and Eric Cantona, it had become mainstream and was losing face with the very crowd who had helped to make it a glamorous brand in the first place.

What's more, allegations about its use of sweatshops continued to linger, while other sports brands such as Adidas and Puma were finding more innovative ways to appeal to Nike's core customer.

Yet Nike had heritage on its side, embodied in Just Do It, one of the world's most famous taglines. Just Do It was created in 1988 by Dan Wieden of Wieden+Kennedy, Nike's agency since 1982, and has proved to have the stamina of a world-class athlete.

Dave Droga, the Creative Chairman of Droga5, sums up the statement's appeal: 'Everyone knows it and it is personalized by consumers. You could be an American athlete wanting to beat a personal best, or a couch potato who's considering walking to the corner shop instead of driving. It's relevant to anybody because it's not too prescriptive.'

Through its swoosh and its slogan, Nike has created a global sporting community. This community was particularly clear in Nike's 2006 World Cup marketing strategy. Nike partnered Google to launch Joga.com, aka 'the community for soccer players dedicated to keeping the game beautiful'. A message on the site reads:

> Joga is about getting to know your fellow fans; creating games and clubs; accessing athletes from Nike; and enjoying video clips and photos (you can even upload your own). You can strengthen existing friendships and begin new ones, join a wide variety of professional athletes and soccer communities, and even create your own to discuss soccer, exchange tips on the coolest moves, browse through various pitches worldwide, and plan your next game. But most of all, Joga is about 'Joga Bonito' – Portuguese for 'play beautiful.'

Joga.com continued long after the 2006 World Cup had ended. Stanley Holmes's article in *Businessweek* on 24 July 2006, 'It's not a shoe, it's a community', reported:

> It's a huge U-turn for the mighty marketer – and a recognition that it needs to get consumers' attention in entirely new ways beyond blasting top-down mass messages… Says Trevor Edwards, Nike's vice-president for global brand management: 'Gone are the days of the one big ad, the one big shoe, and the hope that when we put it all together it makes a big impact.'

By the end of the tournament, 1 million members had registered with Joga.com, but Joga Bonito extends beyond the core website. JogaTV is a virtual soccer TV station for which Nike creates original content, and the sports brand also distributes video clips on content-sharing sites such as YouTube.com. Such relationship building with sports fans gives Nike a special place within their community and has helped it to maintain its competitive advantage.

In addition to taking advantage of new touchpoints and world-class advertising that is a frequent front-runner at awards shows, Nike was quick to pick up on the idea of experience within the retail space. The first Nike Town store opened in Portland, Oregon, in 1990. Others followed.

Nike Town quickly became a destination store on the day it opened. Dermot Cleary, Marketing Director of Nike UK, commented in *Marketing* on 16 September 1999: 'Nike Town is a place where people can experience the brand first hand. Research shows that the average consumer spends 45 minutes in Nike Town. To grab that kind of attention from consumers in any medium is unusual.'

Nike attracted negative publicity around its use of sweatshops, so it has paid more attention to ethical issues. It has worked towards greater transparency and best practice in its supply chain and has also embraced sustainability issues by launching the Reuse-A-Shoe recycling programme and unveiled its Considered range of footwear, which uses water-based adhesives instead of chemical ones.

It promotes exercise through its 10K runs and embeds itself into the running community by encouraging runners to share their best routes online. When runners participated in a 10K run in London in 2005, they were invited to see themselves crossing the finishing line via the internet or 3G phones. It is these details – and the seamless way in which new touchpoints have organically become part of Nike's armoury – that give it such kudos. Not everything pivots on the brand's advertising – indeed, Nike did not run a single TV ad until its sales reached $1 billion. As Nirmalya Kumar points out (2004: 192): 'Up until that milestone, it relied upon "word-of-foot" advertising – getting world class athletes to wear its products.'

Brands that can attract that kind of publicity via brand evangelists *and* that can produce show-stopping ads in a variety of platforms as well as offering opportunities for engagement are in a fundamentally good place.

Case study: Hewlett-Packard – Creating HyPe

When Hewlett-Packard's chief executive, Carly Fiorina, took the top job in 1999, she wanted to rejuvenate HP from a tired brand into a dynamic one that would galvanize it into being the world's most valuable technology brand. Since its merger with Compaq in 2002, HP's positioning had been 'HP Invent' and then '+HP'.

In 2004, HP's HyPe campaign demonstrated a new bravery, as well as a departure in creative and media thinking. Targeting design students, graphic designers and younger creative people coming into the workplace, HP had never really appealed to this group before. HP had always stood for conformity in the eyes of this crowd, who were fiercely defensive of their Macs; the brand was irrelevant to them.

The creative idea behind the campaign was to tap into the deep-seated desire of this group to be noticed, because all young creatives are looking to get their first break. HP decided to create a competition where everybody could create their own work and hang it in the HP gallery. The only requirement was for the work to contain the letters 'H' and 'P'.

In London, young hopefuls could print out their work on a large-format HP printer and then hang it on the gallery walls in Brick Lane. Derek Morris, the Vice-Chairman of ZenithOptimedia in the UK – HP's media agency – describes the gallery as 'art's equivalent to an open mic night at a comedy club'.

Graffiti, posters, postcards and online animations with strange names such as Hairy People and Heavenly Pits started appearing. Thirteen short films from young, unorthodox directors were shown in art-house cinemas, and ads ran in titles like *Sleazenation* and *Dazed & Confused*.

Some 2,500 pieces of creative work by aspiring artists were shown at the gallery, and new spaces subsequently opened in Paris, Barcelona, Milan, Moscow and New York.

Dave Droga, the Creative Chairman of Droga5, comments: 'It snowballed; it didn't do a tap dance to find its audience or hop around pop culture. It initiated something.'

HP also partnered London's National Gallery, and was the first advertiser to erect posters outside the building. The partnership performed a dual function: promoting its role in the preservation of famous works to a business audience, while offering consumers the opportunity to print out their favourite paintings – using an HP printer – inside the gallery.

The HyPe campaign helped HP to become a more consumer-facing global brand. In Germany, Japan, Korea, France, the UK and the United States, it enjoyed double-digit growth.

Olivier Altmann reflects:

After HyPe, the brand image the design community had of HP was totally different. The brand had stopped trying to look hip and trendy by doing advertising that didn't suit its DNA, and instead did something real that was really engaging. HyPe was concrete proof of what it stood for within the creative community. It established a strong bond between those people and the brand and did so much more than any regular advertising could have achieved.

Case study: Unilever – Axe, man's best friend

The Unilever brand Axe – which is known as Lynx in the UK, Ireland and Australia – is one of the world's most popular male grooming products. It's no coincidence that its advertising has attracted 10 Cannes Lions with emotive spots such as 'Getting dressed', which shows a couple locating their strewn clothes following a passionate encounter after a chance meeting in a supermarket.

But Axe goes way beyond advertising; it connects with consumers. In Chapter 7, we showed how Lynx Pulse enjoyed success by working across several channels, and there are many more examples of how it connects in an original and engaging way. Perhaps the most ambitious to date was its intention to launch its own airline, Lynx Jet, in Australia, through a collaborative effort between its agencies Lowe and Universal McCann. Launched through TV, online, retail and field marketing activity, the airline's stewardesses made striking brand ambassadors in their figure-hugging bright yellow uniforms. Passengers travelling on the frequent flyer programme – the Lynx Jet Mile High Club – also got to enjoy pillow fights between the stewardesses, an in-flight hot tub, on-demand spanking sessions and a full body massage.

Adam Lance (2006), the Creative Director at Lowe Hunt in Sydney, which created the campaign, wrote:

> When it was finally time to put our seat back, relax and nibble on a small packet of nuts, we found we had an idea that was ultimately executed through 32 channels. There were TV and radio campaigns, DM pieces, airport posters, print ads, web and ambient ideas, a gorgeous flight crew... The talk the campaign created was immediate and intense. For a while we were in the paper, on TV or on talkback radio every day... Young guys loved the campaign. They dedicated dozens of blog sites to it. But best of all they went out and bought Lynx. 'Jet', the variant we created, became the fastest ever seller in the country and the campaign helped the brand to a record 84.2 per cent share of the category, a jump of 14.1 per cent.

Even though the brand has been in the United States only since 2002, it claimed the category lead of male-targeted deodorants and anti-perspirants in May 2006, according to Mintel. And it has used techniques beyond traditional advertising to achieve that in just four years.

Axe has used viral campaigns all over the world, but it relied entirely on this medium to establish itself in the United States. The launch viral campaign showed the good and bad side of 'man's essence'; our hero's behaviour is shown in a textbook 'good' way, before the film is rewound to show the same action but in a slightly devilish 'bad' way. The film attracted 700,000 unique visitors in the first month and 500,000 of them were not referred via banner advertising, suggesting a high 'forward' rate.

More recently, the brand launched the Gamekillers, a reality show aired on MTV. The gamekillers – a collective noun for those characters who scupper the pulling chances of the Axe target audience – include the mother hen and the drama queen. The campaign was brought to life in bars, college campuses and military bases across the United States.

Axe has also been excellent at engaging through coffee-break fun. On sites across the globe, men can take quizzes to see how proficient they are when it comes to getting the girls, and can also while away the hours tickling a girl with a big feather. Axe really knows its market and it shows in the results: having launched in France over 20 years ago in 1983, Axe is now proving irresistible to men – and women – in more than 60 countries. Unilever also keeps the product fresh by continuing to innovate with new variants.

We chose to focus on the above examples because they are brands that are household names all over the world with one thing in common: they have all invested in engaging with their audience and enjoyed considerable profits as a result. There is nothing special about them; any product can do what they have done. Below we list five ways in which marketing portfolio managers can use experience and engagement to improve their ROI.

ENCOURAGING CONSUMERS TO PARTICIPATE

A momentous media development in the last decade has been reality TV. The likes of *Big Brother* and *Pop Idol* have transformed passive viewers into participants of TV shows, and this development has found its way into advertising.

User-generated content – where brands encourage consumers to interpret the brand – is becoming a popular way for brands to engage. The mayonnaise brand Hellmann's, for instance, launched a sandwich-design competition where the winner nets a share of the profits if the sandwich goes on sale. Meanwhile, the Converse Gallery shows short films contributed by consumers, and MTV's starzine encouraged viewers to 'snap, send and shine'. They could take photos on their mobile phones, send them in via computer or phone, and then design their own magazine layout using their own pictures and copy. Tag Heuer invited consumers to design a website for the watch brand, while Absolut vodka invites artists and designers to interpret the distinctively shaped bottle as part of their creations.

'IN THE FLESH' APPEARANCES

Beer brands are particularly adept at engaging consumers because they can take advantage of the opportunity to be out alongside them. Budweiser, despite spending 60 per cent of its marketing budget on TV, uses a large proportion of the remainder on engagement. So as well as spending money on TV ads around the Super Bowl, Bud and Bud Light are at the event itself, most recently accompanied by the Bud Light mascot, Ted Ferguson, Bud Light Daredevil. The character was reportedly mobbed by fans and even had quarterbacks asking for his autograph.

MAKING IT PERSONAL

When customers are given the red-carpet treatment, they're more likely to return again and again. Having their name and their product preferences remembered makes any customer feel valued. Amazon.com understands this and not only welcomes customers by name but also makes suggestions for their shopping basket based on the products they have bought during that visit.

WHAT'S IN A NAME

When Orange launched in the UK, it was at a time when its competitive set included companies called Mercury, Cellnet and Vodafone. By calling itself something distinctive and having an attention-grabbing slogan – 'The future's bright, the future's orange' – the phone company instantly marked itself out as a creative brand that was somehow different from the rest. It intrigued customers and gave itself a distinctive look and feel. If convention is flouted from the start, the brand will stand much more of a chance of making an impact long-term.

REVAMPING A FLAGGING BRAND

Brands that have been floundering can often enjoy a return to form by learning how to engage. This was the situation in which Kodak found itself. Having been so well known for its film product, Kodak's stock price had plummeted in a world where digital photography was taking off, and it needed to change.

In 2004, it conceived the Kodak Gallery as an engaging communications idea. TV ads showcased Kodak's digital camera – the EasyShare One wifi model, which enables users to e-mail pictures directly from the camera – and a gallery with blank white walls that served as a canvas for pictures. Actual galleries opened in New York and San Francisco that allowed visitors to try out the EasyShare One for themselves by taking pictures and sending them via e-mail. They could also bring in traditional-film pictures to be scanned and converted into digital photos. TV ads backed up the experience and had an impact of 37 per cent, while sales shot up by 50 per cent. Suddenly, Kodak was a hot brand again.

John Hegarty believes that, despite employing elements of science, marketing remains more of an 'art'. He adds that advertising strategies need to rely on sound judgement calls, and concludes that marketing's 'art' status mustn't pigeon-hole it as a frivolous activity.

In 'Why it pays to watch the ads', his column in the *Guardian* on 29 November 2004, Hegarty wrote: 'It must always be remembered that advertising is an investment, just like a new factory or delivery system. I would argue that if you can't promote a compelling advertising strategy and have it executed with consistency, you probably should not be running a company.'

Consistency is one of the biggest ways in which a product can appeal to a consumer. Just Do It and The Axe Effect provide a firm springboard for Nike and Axe to engage with consumers. Nike and Axe have befriended their target audience by being inspirational, interesting and opinionated. They continue to invest in a positive message.

In others words, they are the Beatles *and* the Stones.

10

Apply a 'focus investing' approach

Throughout this book we have talked about applying an investment approach to marketing. For this chapter, we propose applying one of Wall Street's most successful investment strategies.

THE BUFFETT STYLE OF INVESTING

Warren Buffett has been described by the website salon.com as 'the greatest stock market investor of modern times'. He is one of the world's most successful investment managers and frequently introduced as a stock market guru. He runs the fund management company Berkshire Hathaway, and *Forbes* magazine ranks him as the richest person in the world after Bill Gates.

His skill at being able to generate a return on investment is the stuff of legends. Over a 10-year period, he achieved returns that were 10 times higher than the Dow Jones Industrial Average for the same period.

Buffett's skill is encapsulated in his observation that only 10 per cent of funds actually beat the average market performance. He attributes this to the fact that many investors diversify. He believes that investors fall into a trap whereby they convince themselves that, through diversi-fying, they are minimizing risk. Rather than regard diversification of investments as the hallmark of an accomplished investor, Buffett thinks that 'wide diversification is only required when investors do not under-stand what they are doing'.

Secondly, investors buy and sell stocks according to what's fash-ionable. When Google was the darling of the stock market, investors were rushing to buy shares, which artificially spiked the price of stock.

Buffett has developed a strategy that he calls 'focus investing', where investors place big bets on high-probability events. He compares it to playing blackjack; you double your bet once you know you have a good chance at a hand.

Buffett does his homework and considers each investment carefully; he doesn't fall victim to the trends of the stock market, but sticks to his preferred fundamentals. He is famous for buying stocks in companies such as Coca-Cola and Gillette and holding on to them, rather than buying impulsively and changing his portfolio on a regular basis.

FOCUS INVESTING APPLIED TO MARKETING

Buffett's secret weapon is simplicity. In a media landscape with so many available channels, some marketers diversify to cover their bases rather than developing their understanding about the most important drivers for ROI. Marketing portfolio managers need to make clear choices about what is going to lead their communication, which often presents them with one of the hardest decisions on account of the perceived risk of missing something. Yet Buffett has managed to make billions of dollars by doing just that.

The Buffett approach pivots on focusing on a few investments that will deliver the best return.

In our view, diversifying doesn't work in marketing because there is too much noise created by a growing number of media outlets, espe-cially websites, TV stations and magazines. Audiences are fragmenting, so budgets for each touchpoint are diluted. This makes advertising less effective than it used to be because people's attention is dispersed across so many more platforms. Budgets need to be spent differently to stand a chance of being noticed.

Exacerbating the situation is the number of new product launches, partly from existing brands that want to grow additional revenue by venturing into new territory. Ten years ago, who would have been able to predict that Anheuser-Busch, Budweiser's parent company, would unveil 180, an energy drink? The sector didn't even properly exist until Red Bull defined it. And who could have known that the UK super-market chains Tesco and Sainsbury would extend into personal finance, or that Sir Stelios, the founder of the low-cost carrier easyJet, would also launch an easy-branded DVD rental service, pay-as-you-go mobile phones and even a range of male toiletries? The risk of excessive brand extension is that different divisions of a company wind up sending out messages that either add to the clutter or convey a muddled corporate image.

Think of a typical bank promoting insurance policies, credit cards, current accounts, mortgages, loans and pensions – often to the same customer. When all those products are clamouring at once for that customer's attention, their overall impact is diluted.

HOW STRATEGY HELPS FOCUS INVESTING

The essence of strategy is defining how a company is unique and how it will deliver a distinctive mix of value. Strategy is about aligning every activity to create an offering that cannot easily be emulated by competitors. Now is the time for companies to be honest about where they have, or could have, real competitive advantages, and reallocate resources accordingly.

Michael Porter, Professor, Harvard Business School

Porter believes that 'strategy is about making choices and trade-offs; it's about deliberately choosing to be different'. In other words, strategy isn't the art of juggling multiple tasks but focusing on a few. Unfortunately, many companies attempt to be jack of all trades and end up being master of none. Recognizing that they have only limited resources and deciding where to allocate them to achieve maximum payback would be a much easier and more effective way to manage their portfolios.

Porter (2001) suggests that it isn't enough to have a marketing posi-tioning because this can easily be copied by the competition. Instead, there are choices that need to be made with the business to solidify and realize the positioning. By focusing on a strategy and making necessary trade-offs and choices, differentiation will evolve. Articulating clarity, consistency and leadership will also ensure that marketing communications will be more engaging and differentiating. If it achieves this against the desired outcomes, the opportunity for Marketing ROI significantly increases.

To refer back to one of our Marketing ROI stars, O2's strategy in 2005 shifted to focus on customer retention rather than acquisition. By being proactive and single-minded, O2 differentiated itself in the market and showed that it was committed to its customers and confident in its ability to deliver. This strategy was quickly adopted by other operators, but their communications suffered by virtue of being a 'me-too'; they simply didn't have the same focus and therefore resonance as O2.

Marketing could learn from successful business case studies. The example of Enterprise Rent-A-Car shows how, when it focused on a tightly defined market at the beginning, a slow and steady stream of core customers enabled the business to grow organically. Similarly, if marketing campaigns target too broad an audience across too many platforms, they will end up being noticed by no one: the most costly kind of marketing mistake there is.

Case study: Enterprise – The power of being focused

Enterprise Rent-A-Car is the biggest car rental company in North America. Over four consecutive years, it scooped the JD Power and Associates survey, usurping its better-established competitors like Hertz and Avis. Enterprise focused on short-term and replacement rentals rather than following the herd and trying to capture the broader business market. Its focus, along with a strong service ethic, enabled it to charge a premium and, having built up a loyal following of customers, it began appearing in airports in 1998 and is now on-site at 125 across the United States. It made a success of that too – in its tenth annual business travel awards published on 4 January 2003, *Entrepreneur* magazine named Enterprise best rental company, explaining: 'Its success at airport locations is largely due to a winning combination of unique customer service and low rates, which usually run about 20 per cent less than its competitors.'

UNDERSTANDING WHY MARKETING CAMPAIGNS FAIL

Copernicus Marketing Consulting collected performance data on over 500 marketing programmes for consumer and business-to-business products and services. The firm found that 84 per cent of these programmes were decidedly second-rate. Instead of achieving the desired effect of driving value throughout the organizations, they were in fact leading to declines in market share.

There are a number of reasons for such a high rate of failure, which can largely be explained by a lack of focus:

- *Poorly allocated or inefficient spending.* Most campaigns are spread across too many communications channels. An ability to find the more effective channels in a portfolio and to focus on them simply creates value rather than waste. In this scenario, the economies of scale from media buying are lost, alongside an opportunity to maximize an expertise specialization – for instance, 'owning' a particular channel or creating a media 'first'. When spending is inefficient, there is too little frequency, repetition and consistency. What's more, over time the negotiation leverage with channels and suppliers becomes weaker.
- *Ill-defined targeting.* Without regular opportunities to connect with consumers – and by trying to target too many with blanket executions – a campaign will fail. The worst-case scenario is when marketers find they are targeting the wrong consumers with the wrong messages.
- *Weak positioning.* So many products vie to show off how premium they are and what good value they offer that consumers aren't given a chance to learn how they are truly different. Not focusing your message across particular marketing channels can cause a brand to be unclear about what it stands for.
- *Mediocre advertising.* When a campaign fails to stand out with a distinctive message, it's no surprise if a product or service ends up losing market share as opposed to driving it. An ad needs to be memorable if a consumer is going to act upon it. This often means sticking out your neck and focusing on one idea rather than bombarding the consumer with every single piece of information about the product.
- *Too many metrics, too little focus.* If it is unclear from the start what the main objective is, it ends up being impossible to determine whether

the campaign is a success or a failure. More resources are wasted because there isn't sufficient focus on the most important outcomes.

NEW PRODUCT INITIATIVES

Companies are increasingly under pressure to innovate as a means of extending their own portfolio of products, boosting potential revenue streams. Ultimately, they invest in new product development to protect their market share, compete for more shelf space and fight off an attack from a rival product. Companies like to be seen to innovate and like to chase the promise of higher margins. They're also keen to unveil the next star product.

From a PR point of view, innovations make great news stories, while scant attention is devoted to companies that keep doing the same things, however brilliantly they may be performing. Internally, new product initiatives attract more attention from managers and investors.

Marketers – who, according to the search consultants Spencer Stuart, stay in any given role for an average of just 22.9 months – want to be associated with launching new products and their accompanying campaigns. When switching jobs, marketers like to offer a tangible claim to fame. More often than not, this entails a launch campaign.

Despite the financial markets' love affair with innovation, it's worth bearing in mind that new product development and focus are awkward bedfellows. Overemphasizing new product innovation can kill focus. It creates complexity within an organization; extra budget has to be found to launch and market a new product, which could cannibalize the popularity of an existing product. This is a pitfall that car manufacturers in particular have to be especially careful to avoid. What's more, there's always the strong likelihood that a new product won't take off: Philip Kotler (2002) estimates that 80 per cent of new packaged consumer products – including brand extensions – fail.

MAKING THE RIGHT CHOICES

Adopting a focus investing strategy in today's environment is a brave approach because it eschews the temptation to want to be seen to do new things. But focus investing is what smart marketing investors do.

Procter & Gamble's Chairman, AG Lafley, steered the organization back to success by focusing on the company's core cash-generating products. When he inherited the hot seat, P&G was a complex organization: he brought it back to basics with a strategy that focused on a few products.

The Buffett approach to investing – where marketers can bet big on high-probability events *à la* Procter & Gamble – helps facilitate choices that, in turn, assist in differentiating products. This offers brands the best chance of being seen, remembered and known for something at the moment of truth when customers are about to make a purchase decision.

IDENTIFYING THE BIG BETS

In this section, we outline 10 different aspects of marketing where being more single-minded has paid dividends for an organization.

1. Focus... on core brands

Buffett's approach is about developing an instinct for recognizing which products are the most worthy candidates for investment. Most marketing budgets are simply not big enough to promote all the products in an organization's portfolio, so marketers need to be able to work out which ones will generate the highest returns for the organization as a whole. There are three ways to approach this:

- *Promote 'hero' brands.* Follow the example set by AG Lafley and maximize resources by targeting your efforts on a shortlist of established products. By focusing on P&G's global flagship brands such as Olay and Always, the company grew so much that it was able to buy Gillette.

    Apple has also benefited from the success of its iPod: when the Apple store opened on London's Regent Street, 5,000 people turned up. How many would have come to see the store being opened without the iPod taking centre-stage?
- *Use the halo effect of brands.* In the car industry, many marketers will produce a head-turning vehicle that will boost enthusiasm for the mother brand. A by-product of Lexus advertising is that it helps the

Toyota brand. While Lexus is a distinct marque in its own right – appealing to a more elite customer base than Toyota – Toyota drivers benefit from the 'halo' effect, with the knowledge that the two brands share the same engineering.

● *Concentrate on the profit drivers.* Ten years ago, Nestlé marketed more than 8,000 brands in 190 countries. Around 55 were global brands, 140 were regional brands and the remaining 7,800 were local brands. Yet most of the company's profits came from just 200 brands, or just a 2.5 per cent sliver of the entire Nestlé pie. Concentrating on the profit drivers rather than trying to market everything makes it easier to focus.

2. Focus... on core target markets

In 'The Doorman', an episode of *Seinfeld*, Kramer invents a male bra based on the logic that he'll be able to double the size of the bra market. In the Marketing ROI world, the opposite logic applies.

Marketers have only a limited budget, so they need to concentrate on the customer targets that are going to make the biggest difference.

There are a few ways to ensure you're focusing on your target market. One is to avoid the temptation of running with blanket communications that fail to capture anyone's interest.

In the UK, AA loans slimmed down its list of prospects to target used-car buyers rather than general car owners. It successfully positioned the AA as *the* company to turn to for customers seeking to raise funds to buy a used car. Some 34 press executions in 67 titles reached the target market, and AA grew its market share by 150 per cent.

Virgin Mobile also attracted more custom when it chose to define its audience as 16- to 24-year-olds. While its competitive set continued to mass-market, Virgin Mobile realized that it would be more profitable to be more specific. It piggybacked T-Mobile's infrastructure, kept communications relevant to teens and twenty-somethings and enjoyed an impressive return: its market share among that market increased from 34 to 47 per cent as a result.

Another way to focus on a target market is to reach them via their 'influencers', in other words a tight nucleus of people who can help to sell a brand on the marketer's behalf by imbuing it with a certain appeal that makes it attractive to others. Rheingold Beer used this tactic to make its grand return on to New Yorkers' radars.

Case study: Rheingold Beer – Minimum budget, maximum impact

The Lower East Side, East Village and Williamsburg are three New York neighbourhoods that attract a hip crowd who drink 'unmarketed' beer brands. Influencers in these three areas had already worked wonders for fashion brands such as Converse and Levi's.

Rheingold identified 15 'alpha' bars where this crowd drank, and then sponsored an indie music festival where it gave away free beers, and staged events with carefully chosen partners such as the underground magazine *Vice*. It then invested in two well positioned billboards and posted photographs of Rheingold events in full swing around the city.

The *Onion* and the *Village Voice* featured 'Rheingold Picks', which promoted bands playing at Rheingold events – and which now feature on Rheingold's website too. It also featured a happy hour, lasting from 2 am to 4 am, when the beer was half-price. Rheingold reintroduced its famous beauty pageant, but this time only workers from the alpha bars could compete and were judged not so much on their looks, but on their 'raw energy and embodiment of the brand'.

Throughout 2002, the beer enjoyed a distribution increase from just seven bars to 2,000 locations throughout New York. Sales increased every month, resulting in a year-on-year increase of 2,500 per cent.

3. Focus... on communications activity

One of our Marketing ROI stars, O2, is a shining example of how to focus on communications activity. It runs one campaign idea at a time, bucking the trend in its sector to have different ads appealing to a range of customer segments, such as businesses, existing customers and – most commonly – potential customers.

Whether O2 is promoting a new service (such as street maps direct to handsets or its mobile internet function), free minutes, free texts or its capability to serve business customers, the same message appears across a variety of channels, with each touchpoint reinforcing the others. O2's distinctive bubbles assist in giving the brand focus, prompting creativity in the media strategy.

4. Focus... on messaging

There is a strong temptation for marketers to reach everyone and tell them everything about their product at any available opportunity. Marketers need to resist this temptation; otherwise they will end up communicating nothing to nobody.

Olivier Altmann, the Chairman of the Publicis Worldwide Creative Board and the Executive Creative Director of Publicis Conseil in Paris, comments: 'The more one tries to sell, the less one actually sells.'

Publicis Conseil took the 'less is more' approach for Sara Lee's Wonderbra brand and managed to differentiate its message successfully. Instead of going down the well-trodden route of photographing sexy women wearing the bra, posters instead featured people's reactions, as if the consumer looking at the ad was wearing a Wonderbra. So men gawped and gaped, while women glared and glowered. No product benefits were cited, only press and outdoor were used, and the ad targeted both women who would buy the bra for themselves and men who might buy it for them. The ads have helped to keep Wonderbra front of mind, and avoiding the obvious product shot has given the brand much more attitude.

5. Focus... on key markets

Many organizations – particularly large multinationals – operate country-specific or regional P&Ls. This means that local management will fight tooth and claw to hang on to their budget. Very often marketers are bonused on a local performance rather than on their contribution in fulfilling global objectives. This is a tough organizational challenge to overcome, and makes Samsung's story particularly poignant.

For a detailed account outlining how Samsung restructured and improved its ROI, turn to Chapter 11. In essence, the electronics giant redeployed budgets from large-volume markets such as the United States into high-growth markets such as China and Russia. Its annual sales rose by 25 per cent between 2001 and 2002, from $27.7 billion to $34.7 billion. Net income also rocketed, from $2.9 billion to $5.9 billion.

6. Focus... on a single product

As diversification has become commonplace, having just one brand in your portfolio can work as a differentiator. Since it launched in 1987, Red Bull has built an instantly recognizable product and brand by being distinctive: it comes in one size and has no flavoured variants. Red Bull UK chief Harry Drnec reflected in *Marketing Week* on 11 August 2005: 'We're focused. We don't have a cherry drink, a lemon drink, a big pack, a 500ml or a 300ml. We have one functional product that may not taste as good as others but it works and we market it hard.'

The focus has paid dividends for the drink that gives you wings. It's the clear leader in the energy drinks market with at least a 70 per cent share in the 50 countries where it is on sale. Its worldwide turnover is €1.7 billion; sales in the United States alone increased by 50 per cent in 2004.

Red Bull has expanded into 50 countries and enjoyed double-digit growth off the back of one product alone. Soft drinks giants like Pepsi and Coke have now launched their own energy drinks to try to steal a march on Red Bull, but many experiments have bitten the dust. Burn, Coca-Cola's first attempt, was a damp squib.

In a case study on Red Bull written by Suzy Bashford, the ex-Coca-Cola marketer Phil Roman told *Contagious* magazine in its fourth-quarter issue, 2005: 'All of them have dabbled and struggled and finally failed to say "here's a clear positioning of something that's different and here's why."'

7. Focus... the brand on one message

The combination of core product truths and consistent advertising has allowed certain car brands to 'own' certain equities. For instance, Volvo owns safety, Mercedes owns quality, Toyota owns reliability – and all communications tie into this one, pivotal strength. Even newer brands that grew up in the digital space can boast ownership of one specific area: Google owns search; Amazon owns online book sales; eBay owns auctions. Despite all three having their fair share of competition, the one message that shines through is that each one is an expert of their equity, making them a first port of call.

8. Focus... and stick to the strategy

The brands that continue to perform well are those that have a winning strategy and stick to it and don't become sidelined. Again in a marketing world obsessed with fads and fashion, this is incredibly hard to pull off. Ads for Altoids, for instance, have always referenced the words on every tin 'curiously strong'. Every execution reflects that sentiment, regardless of whether it's an ad for Altoids mints, sours or cinnamon strips.

When a strategy is abandoned, it derails consumers; they no longer feel that they have a solid understanding of a particular brand. Smirnoff's share of the US vodka market peaked at 22 per cent in 1974 and then began to decline. New entrants to market, particularly Absolut and Stolichnaya, were beginning to encroach on its long-held supremacy, a situation further exacerbated by the rise of premium vodkas like Grey Goose and Absolut Level at the start of the new millennium.

Smirnoff's inconsistent advertising was also partly to blame: 14 separate campaigns had run between 1953 and 1994, and each one had a different theme and visual imagery, from 'self-expression' and the Woodstock era to 'reigning vodka', which defensively tried to hold on to the supremacy that Absolut had within its reach.

David A Aaker (1996), Professor Emeritus of Marketing at Berkeley University, reflects: 'Because of the endless changes, it was unclear what Smirnoff stood for. The Smirnoff identity was muddled in terms of its personality, its visual image, its value proposition, and the basis of its relationship with the customer.'

9. Focus... on a single product solution

If it appears as if there is no tangible difference in your product compared with your competitors', marketing portfolio managers need to take responsibility for identifying one. Presenting consumers with a product solution permeates the product with 'must-have' appeal.

When Unilever in Asia developed a microwaveable soup, Soupy Snax, it initially failed to set the world alight. The soup was then relaunched as a healthy energy-boosting snack that could lift lethargic office workers when they began to flag at 4 pm. Sales soared as soon as the brand had been given a purpose via a strong marketing idea.

10. Focus... on a channel strategy

If a brand is spread too thinly across several different touchpoints, it will quickly become wallpaper and fail to be noticed, let alone provide inspiration or a reason for purchase.

That's why many campaigns that stand out have been focused on a particular channel strategy.

Case study: The Economist – White on Red

The Economist's use of outdoor for a business-to-business campaign was an unusual choice in a market that normally relies on the business sections of national newspapers, targeted radio stations and TV news shows.

The use of posters supported the creative insight, which suggested that its readers belong to an elite of successful people. As outdoor is often called 'the last broadcast medium', the fact that the ads were shown to all and sundry actually helped to define this elite and the people who belong to it: the posters immediately appealed to those who 'got' them as much as they bewildered those who didn't.

No other publication has ever used outdoor to the extent that *The Economist* does, effectively allowing it to 'own' the medium in the way that Volvo 'owns' safety (see '7. Focus... the brand on one message').

Poster exposure also enabled creative ideas to be maximized. Sites bought on commuter routes meant that passengers would see the execution every time they travelled to and from work, giving them ample time eventually to understand the message – and experience that self-satisfaction, or even smugness, at 'belonging' to the elite.

Both medium and message reinforced the brand communication, while sites at airports and train stations made the most of their environs with the newspaper's characteristic wit.

Econometric modelling revealed that every £1,000 spent on advertising generates 60 news-stand sales and 6.3 subscriptions. Every year, *The Economist* spends approximately £1 million on the brand campaign, so the advertising generates 60,000 news-stand sales and 6,300 subscriptions, equating to 2.4 per cent of news-stand sales and 5.7 per cent of subscriptions.

The long-running campaign, through Abbott Mead Vickers BBDO, also encourages people to form a loyal relationship with the newspaper by taking out – and continuing to renew – a subscription. In 2005, *The Economist's* global circulation hit 1 million. Advertising, as the econometric modelling indicates, has had a direct effect on circulation. In the same year, the Economist Group's turnover rose to £197 million and profits grew to £27 million.

Source: IPA Effectivenewss Awards, WARC.

MAKING CHOICES ABOUT COMMUNICATION

Sometimes, it's not just about the strategy you employ but how well you execute it. As a case in point, take Heineken and Budweiser in China. Both brands were trying to establish themselves in the imported beer category and were starting from the same situation: they had an equal market share; both of them targeted the same kind of drinker and had similar-sized budgets.

Yet their marketing communications strategies were completely different. Budweiser spent three times the amount that Heineken did on TV. Bud also ran high-profile sponsorships around events such as the World Cup. The US brand relied on the highly creative TV executions from long-term agency DDB to engage with its audience, and there was no mistaking its US heritage.

Heineken, on the other hand, spent about 80 per cent of its budget below the line. It was much more skilled in executing on-premise promotions, working with a specialist integrated marketing agency called 141 to boost its profile in discos and in bars. Heineken's event sponsorships such as the Shanghai Tennis Open tournament and music events reached opinion-formers and proved to be an effective way for the brand to grow its presence.

Both clients were equally good at producing, evaluating and managing their marketing portfolios. While Budweiser's TV advertising was, spot for spot, more effective than Heineken's, outside of that medium the king of beers did not boast the expertise that Heineken had in understanding how to get in front of consumers. In short, neither brand could have successfully executed the other's strategy.

Both Bud and Heineken grew their market share equally successfully as Chinese drinkers sought alternatives to cheaper, local beers, proving that there's no silver bullet for any particular sector; a multitude of different approaches are possible. Instead this is an example of having a clear strategy and focusing all the marketing team's resources in executing it.

BETTING ON BUFFETT

Warren Buffett's success has hinged on buying stocks in which very few other investors are showing any interest. When everyone else was buying technology stocks, he was investing in consumer packaged goods companies; while other fund managers had over 100 companies in their portfolio, he would focus on a mere handful. He's not been afraid to buck trends; his focus has enabled him to stick to his guns and not subject himself to the vagaries of the markets. By doing this, Buffett has made a lot of people a lot of money.

Just like investing in stocks and shares, managing a marketing communications portfolio is not for the faint-hearted. But, by learning from Buffett's extensive experience, marketing portfolio managers can adopt an approach that will help to steer their investments towards profitability.

11

Establish a measurement culture

> The only point of metrics is to build something realistic and practical into the day-to-day running of a business. Metrics should give marketers the information that they need to do things differently to drive progress. If metrics don't do that, remaining in the 'nice to know' box, the problem hasn't been cracked.
>
> Ingrid Murray, Managing Director, Ninah Consulting

Setting up metrics at the start of the investment process is vital if you intend to enjoy a return. Successful investors allocate time to tracking their investments because studying charts and poring over analyses of the market are as important as the ability to research a particular stock in the first place. There is an art to reading charts and staying in touch with the signals that stock is going up or down. By reading the market, investors know exactly when to enter – as well as when to hold back. Most importantly of all, they use data to inform when to make changes in their portfolio.

Investors understand that they are not checking information for the hell of it; they are squeezing it for the intelligence it gives them. Tracking your investments is a worthwhile activity only if you are prepared to act constructively armed with that information.

While there's no doubt that marketing requires a degree of creativity, using data wisely will seriously reduce the risk of ill-informed – and potentially disastrous – decision making.

SETTING OUT THE PROBLEM

Imagine watching a football match where all the analysis happened before the game. Think about it: no commentary during the 90 minutes on the pitch and no post-match analysis.

In traditional marketing management, this scenario is all too common. Ninety per cent of everyone's energies are invested in pre-campaign planning before the first spot appears. All the effort is up front, in analysing the marketing situation, budgeting, developing a strategy, selling it into management, briefing agencies and developing and reviewing the work itself. After the campaign has broken, there is insufficient time and resource dedicated to post-launch or post-campaign analysis before momentum gears up again for the next burst of activity.

Rob Rees, Troubleshooter, Interim Marketing/Commercial Director and Co-Founder of Freestyle Marketing, calls this 'a fire and forget mentality'. He says:

> No one reviews their activities in business because they're too busy going on to the next thing. After a campaign, an appraisal of the market and a post-launch review are crucial. Yet I could count on one hand the number of times I've seen them in action. That's sloppy because it means that money isn't being spent carefully enough, and no learning is being gained along the way.

A six-month study by Wirthlin Worldwide and Atlantic Research in the United States in 2003 shone the spotlight on 135 national campaigns for high-end products and services. It found that 91 per cent of the campaigns reported an increasing importance in demonstrating their ROI. Tellingly, in the same study, 41 per cent perceived their superiors to be dissatisfied with current ROI measurement.

And despite 76 per cent of respondents tracking unaided brand awareness, only 59 per cent considered it a useful metric for ROI. This was typical: only about half of the campaign managers and executives thought that standard metrics were effective in measuring ROI. Again, this raises the question posed in Chapter 5: what is the point of measuring something if the numbers are of little or no value?

A typical situation sees marketers assessing their budget allocation on a yearly basis, but all too often opting to use the same channels instead of changing their investments to improve their return. Eighty-one per cent of marketers say that 'acting quickly to improve results' is 'very' or 'somewhat' difficult (Forrester/ANA, 2004). Yet with digital channels attracting a greater share of budgets, it's never been easier to reassess a campaign and change it, if need be.

In a jaw-dropping example (VanBoskirk, 2005) that demonstrates how making minor tweaks in the middle of a planning cycle can make a massive difference to a campaign, Ford Motors discovered that shifting just a further 2 per cent of its budget into online would generate a return of $90 million in additional profit.

OUR VIEW...

Planning should be a more fluid process with less emphasis on upfront analysis and much more attention to current and post-campaign analysis.

Market intelligence can be a company's competitive marketing advantage. It stands to reason that understanding the market and distinguishing between what is and isn't working can unlock significant Marketing ROI value.

To return to the Wirthlin and Atlantic US study, their findings unearthed a crucial insight into where marketers were going wrong with ROI measurement. There was a direct correlation between those campaigns that had followed a process of identifying, measuring and managing ROI goals and satisfaction with their results. Ninety per cent of campaigns that had incorporated ROI goals into their campaign process reported that senior stakeholders were either somewhat or very satisfied with the final campaign. Yet this figure more than halved – to 44 per cent – among client respondents when there were no ROI goals or process. The report concluded: 'Ad executive and campaign managers who actively manage the ROI process and generate value-building outcomes see the link between improvements in the ROI process and outcomes – those who do not, reluctantly pursue ROI to justify ad spending' (Moore and Allsop, 2004).

Successful campaigns report significantly greater satisfaction with outcomes or ROI tracking not because of preferred technologies, methodologies, greater resources or inherent campaign advantages, but on account of an active and disciplined management of ROI resources. Senior managers frequently display much greater confidence in data when ROI is 'hard-wired' into the process – further proof that data needs to be used to improve and optimize campaigns, not just to evaluate them.

Principles from the worlds of direct and digital marketing could benefit mainstream consumer marketing by being applied to more vigorous market testing of campaigns post-launch – similar to the way in which stock market investors would keep track of their investments. But it's not enough just to gather these data; it's vital to act on them too.

SET METRICS AT THE START

All too often, metrics are used to justify the campaign objectives. This is particularly common when marketers are simply repeating the same investments year after year. In many cases, particularly with newer touchpoints such as the internet, mobile phones and interactive TV, there is only limited access to retrospective data, so marketers are less inclined to include those media in their marketing portfolios. This accounts for the fact that, in the United States, TV CPMs (i.e. the costs of reaching TV audiences) have increased by 68 per cent since 1995 even though TV ad recall has fallen from 40 per cent in 1960 to just 6 per cent in 2003. As Shar VanBoskirk points out, most marketers – 79 per cent – intend to increase their interactive media budgets, but existing systems don't support that intention (VanBoskirk, 2005). This could help to explain why, after a review process with their agencies, many marketers often take the path of least resistance and decide to repeat recent activity.

There's a need to avoid being defensive about ROI. If there was more honesty about marketing's effect and results because metrics and targets were established up front as part and parcel of the campaign's objectives, the ROI would undoubtedly benefit.

The metrics need to be aligned with the business objectives and the key stakeholders. Only then can they can provide a clear focus for the marketing team and the agency to develop the communication. Introducing metrics at the start of the process will lead to better-quality briefs to agencies, which in turn will prompt improvements in insight, strategy and planning. The Lexus case study described in Chapter 5 reported that the brief given by Lexus was to generate more test drives among affluent Europeans. This led to tight targeting – holidaymakers in exclusive destinations – and spawned an original creative idea that generated an impressive return for the client.

When there is more emphasis on metrics at the start of the campaign, senior management will start to regard marketing as more transparent and accountable, helping it to bat off some of the more negative PR that it has attracted over the years.

IT'S NOT FAILURE; IT'S LEARNING

Success represents 1 per cent of your work and results form the 99 per cent that is called failure.

Soichiro Honda, Founder, Honda

If the metrics indicate that the results fall short of original targets, the temptation to write off this process as a 'failure' needs to be resisted. Instead, learn from it and improve it. One of our Marketing ROI stars, Procter & Gamble, has created a strong culture from establishing learning rather than judging results as either a 'success' or a 'failure'. The accumulation of results provides much better insight in setting future goals and understanding the marketing process, so it's important to apply a 'test and learn' approach: success is not guaranteed overnight. This is a cultural shift that may need to be addressed. In one of his lessons, 'Empower your people to deliver', featured on www.50lessons.com, the Vice-President, Sales and Marketing at Microsoft EMEA, Neil Holloway, underlines the advantages of building a learning culture rather than an environment where teams live in constant fear of making mistakes:

With so much at stake from any big decision, how can you create the environment which enables people to make mistakes and still feel they can be part of the overall endgame? Part of that just comes down to judgement. First of all, you have to understand the framework you're creating for people, so people understand what risks they can take and when they need to come for input, and sometimes an ultimate decision. And it's about creating an environment to enable a judgement call: does the action which the person's just done, where they've made a mistake, what are the consequences of that, and how much are you willing to let it ride? Make sure that you go back and do the coaching so the person understands what's just happened. That enables them to continue, compared to: 'Ouch! That's just broken the whole process we were going through here.'

Metrics drive the entire marketing process, and what it is trying to achieve, whether it's acquiring new customers or retaining existing ones. The ability to judge the success of a particular marketing activity in fulfilling a specific business objective is vital if the objective is ever going to be achieved. That includes a mindset that is philosophical rather than one that is quick to dish out blame when the figures fall short of their targets. Armed with that information, action could be taken that might mean that targets are exceeded in the second year of activity.

METRICS: MOVING THE NEEDLE

Collecting and analysing the data backed up by a readiness to change the status quo drive Marketing ROI. The following case study shows how Samsung reviewed its investment portfolio and made some significant changes that helped make the electronics giant generate a considerable return.

Case study: Samsung – Making every dollar count

In their 2003 *Harvard Business Review* paper 'Optimal marketing', Marcel Corstjens and Jeffrey Merrihue explain how, on his arrival at Samsung in 1999, Eric Kim, the Executive Vice-President of Global Marketing, set out with a mission to transform the company. Kim wanted to make Samsung a formidable rival to the industry leader Sony. On a billion-dollar budget, Kim had to allocate resource to reap maximum returns.

Challenge

Samsung was a low-profile brand that was broadly considered to be a low-cost option for PDAs, mobile phones and DVD players. Its primary function historically, though, had been as a supplier of computer monitors and semiconductors to more powerful multinationals. It had to prove that it was not the cheap and cheerful electronics option but a reputable household name that placed a high premium on quality and innovation.

When it came to the thorny issue of how it should invest its billion-dollar budget, Samsung realized it was suffering from an information deficit. Data collection had traditionally been erratic, and was in no coherent state to be helpful as a constructive aid to decision making. Comparisons across regions, for instance, were impossible because data weren't standardized. Samsung had information for fewer than 30 per cent of its category–country combinations, making comparisons such as potential sales of DVD players in the United States against camcorder sales in Japan an impossible task.

Solution

Samsung collated data for different territories in M-Net, its marketing intranet. This included:

- overall population and population of target buyers;
- spending power per capita;
- per capita spending on product categories;
- category penetration rates;
- overall growth of categories;
- share of each of the company's brands;
- media costs;
- previous marketing expenditures;
- category profitability;
- competitor metrics.

It collected benchmark data helping the company to compare its spending per medium with other brands. It also used M-Net as a source for internal expertise.

M-Net data helped Samsung to realize where it was and where it could go by evaluating all potential allocation scenarios that could yield a higher ROI. Reallocation technology was built into M-Net that analysed historical data such as past sales volumes and revenues by product and by country. This meant that Samsung marketing staff could analyse the results of their recent global marketing investments *and* build predictive models that would help them to identify where and how current marketing investments would yield the highest future returns. M-Net also helped answer 'what if?' questions.

M-Net threw up serious mismatches between investment and growth, and revealed three important areas for attention:

1. Forty-five per cent of Samsung's budget was being spent in North America and Russia, yet both markets offered relatively low growth potential. Investment could be pruned by 10 per cent.
2. Samsung was underinvesting in Europe and China, which received 31 per cent of the budget. Based on profit potential, these territories should receive 42 per cent.
3. Half of Samsung's marketing budget was devoted to promoting its mobile phones, vacuum cleaners and air-conditioning units. Investment could be reduced by 22 per cent to support new products.

In short, Samsung would have to reallocate approximately $150 million of its marketing budget from more mature categories and regions to those that offered more potential. The United States, Samsung's largest market, no longer offered the most potential for growth.

Implementing such momentous changes required tact and organization, particularly as local marketing managers would have to become more aware of the bigger picture rather than the performance of their individual business units. How marketing staff were remunerated would also be affected.

Samsung conducted 121 meetings and workshops with its marketing staff to fine-tune its findings and seek out feedback. And to avoid marketing executives feeling hard done by in countries where budget cuts were necessary, Kim and his team met to present the case for budget reallocation in person. Kim told the *Harvard Business Review*: 'In a project such as this, there's no substitute for effective communication when it comes to implementing change… We had to explain what we were doing, why were doing it, and how it was critical to the future success of Samsung globally.'

Samsung successfully minimized resistance and recognized that it had to develop new ways of evaluating, compensating and developing employees who were affected by the changes. For instance, the company began to offer marketing executives more opportunities to work in different market situations, including lower- and higher-growth markets.

Results

Samsung is among the top five leaders in the global market for mobile handsets and has made significant gains in the markets for camcorder, flat-panel computer monitors, DVD players and recorders, and digital TVs – categories that tend to be dominated by Sony. In digital music players it has leapt from tenth to third, from eighth to second in LCD monitors and TVs, and from unranked to eighth in portable DVD players.

Table 11.1 Samsung's allocation process: before and after M-Net

The traditional approach to budgeting and planning	The fact-based approach to budgeting and planning
Category managers campaign for incrementally larger annual marketing budgets.	Critical country and product-category data are collected into M-Net, the company's online marketing data repository.
HQ's marketing management responds based on incomplete information, traditional approach and gut instinct.	Using M-Net's analytical engines, corporate marketers identify high-potential country–category combinations.
Outsized increases go to the biggest markets and 'squeaky wheels'.	What-if scenarios are tested to determine the most effective allocation of marketing resources.
Over- and under-investments are rampant, yet no one knows where or by how much.	The allocation is refined based on insights of field marketing managers, and then finalized by HQ.
Marketing's total budget appears arbitrary and indefensible.	The fact-based case for the allocation is presented in meetings with field managers.
Top management grows increasingly uncomfortable with the overall marketing investment.	Senior management gains confidence in its level of marketing investment.

Source: Corstjens and Merrihue (2003)

Interbrand also estimates that Samsung has been the fastest-growing global brand – its brand value increased 30 per cent between 2001 and 2002 to be worth $8.3 billion. By 2004, the brand was worth $12.6 billion.

Sales at Samsung rose 25 per cent between 2001 and 2002, from $27.7 billion to $34.7 billion, and income by $2.5 billion to $5.9 billion. Samsung is committed to sustaining this growth.

INTRODUCING AN ROI SYSTEM

Julian Elliott, the Group Marketing Head of Effectiveness at Lloyds TSB, uses a powerful analogy to illustrate the random nature of most marketing efforts: 'If you were working in oil or gas exploration and you just started drilling random holes, you'd be fired pretty quickly. In marketing, though, the attitude seems to be "Let's drill a few holes over here" and hang on to a hope that most of them will generate a response.'

Instead of a haphazard approach, marketers need to take into consideration their finite resources – people and time – and keep front of mind that marketing needs to be a source of value creation. Then they can decide where the best places are to drill so that they can give themselves the best possible opportunity of striking oil.

In order to do this, there need to be three attitudinal changes:

- Adopt a measurement mindset.
- Ban marketing myths in your department. Examples include 'You can't measure long-term impact.'
- Don't try to define ROI too literally – the discipline, process and mindset of accountability are what's important in driving more effective marketing strategies.

Steps that Elliott introduced at Lloyds TSB can be summed up by SAM (Spend, Activity, Measure):

- *Spend.* Visibility of the total marketing budgeting needs to be created. The more furtive breed of marketers can harbour a tendency to hide those embarrassing elements of their budgets that aren't working. A culture of transparency needs to be nurtured. In the long term, there's no room for marketers who try to cover their tracks and don't share results. Over time, the pressure on marketers to demonstrate the results of what they do will only increase, so it is within their interests to evolve.

- *Activity.* Evaluate and catalogue which marketing investments are working most effectively. Future budget allocation decisions depend on a combination of more of what's working well now and either eliminating or substantially reducing underperforming investments.
- *Measure.* Once you have worked out where the marketing budget is being allocated, measure all the different elements, so you can link the results back to spend. You can then be informed about where you are putting your budgets for the coming year and can confidently move spend into those areas that have the best chance of success.

It is usually more profitable to support proven copy, strong regions or particular targets than building up weak areas. Refer back to the 80/20 rule: keep investing 80 per cent of your budget on what's working, and save 20 per cent for experimentation. Focus on the strengths rather than trying to 'correct' the weaknesses.

Evidence of ROI in action

Procter & Gamble, the US telecom AT&T, Nestlé, Johnson & Johnson, Kraft and other big marketers claim to have made great strides in understanding how their marketing strategies have affected their bottom lines. P&G is even said to have changed how it spent over one-tenth of its global marketing budget based on marketing-mix modelling. However, even the progress that they have made is not extensive enough. As Frank Harrison, Strategic Resources Director for ZenithOptimedia Worldwide, says: 'I don't think there's a marketer on earth who could claim to have cracked ROI.'

MODELLING

Modelling measures consumer sales response to marketing activity and, just as with metrics, numbers gleaned from models are only useful if they can be interpreted and used in some way to inform future decision making.

More marketers will realize the benefits of using market-mix models or lifetime value as reliable metrics; in time, these metrics are likely to eclipse analysis reports or attitude and usage studies.

This growing reliance on modelling requires greater commitment and resources. An organization that wants to use modelling more needs to invest in it, perhaps assigning a marketer who will disseminate results through the organization. In the United States, the likes of McDonald's, Procter & Gamble and Comcast have all hired staff with specific responsibility for modelling.

The advantages of modelling

- It can complement the portfolio approach because it takes into account external factors such as other market activity, including a 'halo' marketing effect. For instance, advertising a regular fizzy drink brand will drive sales of the diet variety, while mobile handset brands will invest in marketing their most innovative models, which will drive sales of their less sophisticated ranges.
- It determines budgets. Ninah Consulting worked with Lexus Europe, which wanted to be as big in Europe as it is in the United States. Lexus headquarters in Japan turned down Lexus Europe's initial budget request. Modelling in Germany and the UK looked at how new models had performed, the competition (other luxury brands such as Mercedes and BMW) and Lexus's market positioning in the United States and how that had been achieved. Following six weeks of looking at data, Ninah recommended that in fact Lexus needed to increase its budget in Europe by a further 60 per cent over the original budget set. Ingrid Murray reflects: 'This was not about persuading Lexus to run with a creative idea; it was more about persuading them to run with a strategy.'
- It can help to determine where the budget should be allocated, for instance in regional or national media. MasterFoods, for example, runs regional testing for its media campaigns: in one region it will run a TV campaign, while another works as a control. It will test the outcome on its sales figures to determine the effect that, for example, TV advertising is having. As long as everything in the two selected regions remains largely static, this can be an effective way for the consumer packaged goods companies to have access to data that

can inform future marketing strategies. For MasterFoods and other companies that invest in being informed, that experience constitutes a major competitive advantage.

- It indicates incremental sales. Over half of all sales occur without marketing, according to Jim Nail, so modelling helps to isolate the effect of marketing versus other factors, for instance the weather or pricing. Nail points out that a heatwave could boost sales of soft drinks, while hikes in fuel prices have muted consumer enthusiasm for SUVs (Nail, 2005).

- It compares commercial effectiveness. One ad may be particularly more powerful than others for the same product, and modelling can single out the magic execution. A haircare brand that ran 13 different commercials found the most popular was 220 per cent more effective than the weakest. Increasing the investment behind the most effective copy increases the performance of the total portfolio.

OWNING ECONOMETRICS

It's natural for marketers' first reaction to be to resist metrics, perhaps fearing that the numbers will say something that won't fit with their agenda.
Ingrid Murray, Managing Director, Ninah Consulting

Owning the modelling process is vital; otherwise it risks becoming one of those 'to-do' items that gets shunted around, and no one takes ultimate responsibility for it. With an assigned person being responsible for implementing the findings, modelling can start to show the tangible business benefits listed above.

Julian Elliott, the Head of Group Marketing Investment at Lloyds TSB, estimates that one of his main tasks is to persuade his colleagues that modelling does work. He reveals: 'There were times when we tried to build econometric modelling systems only to be told "We don't need one of those." We retorted: "How are you going to predict next year's sales then?"'

Outside of consumer packaged goods sectors there's a lack of awareness in the marketing community that econometric tools exist and, even when that isn't the case, there is limited knowledge about what the tools can do for a business. The best of all worlds is when someone owns and drives the modelling process internally and combines that responsibility for it with the knowledge and experience of the people who understand the brands involved best. That way, the richness of information gleaned about customer behaviour and attitudes towards the brand and competitor brands can complement scientific data, which can then inform investment decisions.

One of the limitations of econometrics is that it uses historical data. While it provides valuable measurement of what best works in the current environment, econometric modelling isn't able to predict results in changing marketing conditions. Ninah Consulting is one of a number of companies that is an exception to the rule because it combines historical analysis with facilitated management judgement. The resulting model is 'owned' and understood by the client, and provides the 'what if?' capability to analyse the impact of brand investment decisions on short- and long-term sales, profit and ROI.

Murray says: 'Econometric modelling enables you to build an accurate picture of how each activity impacts brand performance because the conclusions are mathematically substantiated.'

The downside, she adds, is the investment of time and money required by marketers who want to use econometrics: results can take up to four months to be delivered, and an econometric modelling system involves a large initial outlay. But isn't finding the time and the money worth it, especially if it means more appropriate marketing choices are being made?

MARKETING DASHBOARDS

One metric on its own is not enough. Instead, using several metrics that combine to form a marketing dashboard can be a much more effective way of tracking your investments and how well they are working. This was certainly the case for Unisys according to a paper published in the *Journal of Advertising Research* in September 2004 by Amy Miller and Jennifer Cioffi entitled 'Measuring marketing effectiveness and value: the Unisys marketing dashboard'.

Case study: Unisys – The marketing dashboard

Unisys, the information technology services and solutions company, found that introducing a marketing dashboard had wide-ranging benefits for measuring marketing's contribution to business performance, according to Miller and Cioffi. The dashboard concept is becoming more common in the IT marketplace, particularly for global corporations like Unisys whose marketing coverage spans over 100 countries and targets clients in financial services, transportation, communications, the public sector and commercial/media.

Challenge

Prior to 2003, Unisys had no single system to measure its Marketing ROI. Its structure, operations and culture meant that 'marketing' meant either global marketing or corporate communications, while marketing activity was conducted within regional marketing groups and four business units. No marketing measurement systems were coordinated across different divisions, hindering big-picture analysis or insight. Management couldn't identify business practices or roles that weren't growing the company's value, nor could management evaluate marketing performance. Unisys's decentralized marketing organization meant that marketing budgets were managed within six distinct units, which set their own goals and strategies.

Solution

In 2002, Unisys launched an integrated, real-time, online marketing dashboard with help from Venture Communications and the Information Technology Services Marketing Association (ITSMA). The dashboard allowed Unisys to achieve the following:

- Common goals and objectives for marketing operate across all the Unisys business units.
- The six primary marketing organizations at Unisys can holistically view performance against programme goals. Together, they form a consolidated dashboard that can be used in the boardroom and by the CEO.
- Marketers can manage programmes in real time on an ongoing basis and make any changes immediately.
- Senior management reporting provides clear, tangible evidence of the value marketing delivers and its contribution to overall business impact.
- Marketing and sales alignment is strengthened.
- Unisys drives disciplined decision making.

The requirements for the marketing dashboard were that it should be:

1. *simple:* the system had to be easy to understand and straight-forward to implement;
2. *inclusive:* key marketing players had to support and be involved with the system;
3. *quantitative:* the system needed to focus on quantitative metrics, although not exclude qualitative metrics;
4. *flexible:* the system had to be future-proof (as far as possible) for Unisys as an organization;
5. *compatible:* the system had to ensure that it aligned all key goals, objectives, activities and metrics;
6. *exemplary:* best practice insights had to be built into the system;
7. *bespoke:* the system had to reflect the corporate structure and strategic direction of Unisys.

Results

The dashboard was tested with the launch of a services solution in summer 2003. It rose to the challenge, providing management with instant access to marketing performance and an ability to track results set against targets for revenue, brand awareness and press coverage.

The dashboard provided real-time performance data to help keep marketing on track. It offered insights to marketing executives so they could make fact-based decisions that allow them to allocate future resources based on what's working and what's not. It helped the marketing team to synchronize its activities across the organizations, and to track progress made towards key objectives.

It is regarded as the driver of operational effectiveness, helping everyone at Unisys to speak the same language in terms of goals and objectives. It has also helped to convince the cynics that marketing is a business enabler.

Unisys has set the standard for what has become a recognized industry best practice for implementing marketing dashboards in large-scale, complex IT companies.

MARKET TESTING

Twenty per cent of my time is spent on numbers. Most of it is spent running test programmes.

Julian Elliott, Lloyds TSB

Remember in Chapter 4 where we recommended the investment strategy of 80/20, where 80 per cent of the budget is spent on 'bankers' that are guaranteed to deliver a return, while the remaining 20 per cent is set aside for media and messaging tests and experimentation?

Traditionally, communication channel planners revisit their communications plan annually and continue to plan and buy the channels with which they feel most comfortable. This approach allows for very little testing or adjustment as changes in market conditions or customer behaviour emerge.

Instead, marketers and their agencies could learn from digital planning processes: rather than place large upfront deals in advance, they could consider buying in small blocks. They could then enjoy the flexibility of measuring and optimizing their campaigns rather than waiting for weeks or months following the end of a campaign to receive results that indicate whether it's been a success or not.

DATA, NOT DINNER

There will be other, more cultural consequences of marketers placing more emphasis on data, according to Shar VanBoskirk's (2005) report *Left Brain Marketing Planning*. Budget allocation decisions will pivot on media performance rather than the relationships between buyer and seller, while agencies will invest in strategy and analytics staff rather than deal makers. VanBoskirk sounds the death knell for what she calls 'the schmooze factor': 'A few more box seats at the Lakers game and corner tables at The Plaza will sit empty as media companies and agencies use data – not wining and dining – to win dollars from Left Brain Marketers.'

The future belongs to the data-heads.

12

Leverage your employee capital

Broadly speaking, we're all more or less happy with the products that are produced, but everybody's deeply dissatisfied with almost every service that exists... Why? Because running a service business is infinitely more complicated than running a product business. In the service business, the people who matter – the people who communicate the brand idea – are the most junior employees because those are the people you deal with.

Wally Olins, CBE, Chairman, Saffron (2006: 60–61)

INVESTING IN STAFF...
TO INVEST IN CUSTOMERS

Throughout this book, we have applied an investment approach to marketing, suggesting that adopting such a mindset will help organizations become more ROI-smart and profit-focused. In this chapter, we suggest that it's easy to create advertising that damages a company's reputation by over-promising.

A significant number of highly effective campaigns tend either to target employees directly or to leverage staff as part of marketing initiatives. This chapter is devoted to four particularly persuasive examples.

These examples show that such a strategy does not have to result in dry communication: far from it. When Honda's communication finally found its voice, staff turnover rates dropped from 11 per cent to 7 per cent between 2002 and 2005 in the UK. In the same period, sales rose by 28 per cent. Such an impressive performance seems to suggest that marketing and HR need to work more closely together and share common needs rather than remaining in their silos.

It's particularly vital that service brands pay attention to bringing their staff with them through their communications because, when you're buying a service, you're buying people. A BrandAsset Valuator USA study compared goods with services brands. In each category – differentiation, relevance, esteem and knowledge – the goods brands outperformed the service brands, with differentiation performing particularly weakly.

Good service can be a key differentiator. Ian Batey of Batey Advertising invented the Singapore Girl for Singapore Airlines, where real-life stewardesses were used to emphasize the premium in-flight service of the airline. Potential stewardesses applying for jobs with the airline knew what was expected of them from the advertising, and customers could look forward to high standards of service. The Singapore Girl idea is now over 30 years old and continues to embody the essence of the airline.

Addressing employees via appropriate communications should be a fundamental marketing objective, not a bonus outcome.

McDonald's understands this. The retailer recognizes that, while a customer may see up to three minutes of advertising for the Golden Arches in an average week, that same customer has up to 15 extra minutes of advertising 'air-time' while waiting in-store for food. How the employee interacts with the customer makes up a vital element of that experience.

It's a virtuous circle. If you invest correctly and sensibly in communicating with your staff, your return will improve. Richard Branson has built up his Virgin empire on the logic that happy workers create happy customers, and good customer experiences inevitably lead to happy shareholders.

Strong service brands attract high-calibre candidates for jobs and decent suppliers because they can imagine the kudos that the association will bring. Having distinctive communications that both build a brand and appeal to staff is a form of leadership that acts as a rallying cry across an organization.

BP's 'Beyond Petroleum' is one such example. Speaking to *Chief Executive* in December 2003, Shelly Lazarus, the CEO of Ogilvy, BP's agency, comments:

Having a clear brand message can be an effective way to create coherence around a complex set of ideas, and it can create a common bond that can give any company a truly competitive advantage. Lord John Browne [the outgoing chief executive] of BP is using his brand brilliantly to get his people focused on the next chapter for his company. In a world where energy will always be needed, BP is moving Beyond Petroleum to meet that need. Two small words define the brand and tell the world, and BP's own people, where the future lies.

But, as anyone who has had a bad call centre experience will no doubt relish admitting, there is a lot of work to be done. A study by Walker Information and Hudson Institute revealed the following findings from a US survey (Lowenstein, 2003). It's depressing reading:

- Only 24 per cent of employees considered themselves truly loyal and committed to their organization and its goals, and planned to stay at least two years.
- There were 33 per cent of employees who were high-risk, not committed and not planning to stay.
- There were 39 per cent who were classified as trapped.
- Among those who felt they worked for an ethical organization, 55 per cent were truly loyal. For those who didn't feel they worked for an ethical organization, the loyalty figure was 9 per cent.

If marketing communication can hit the right tone, it can endorse the workplace for employees while also presenting an attractive proposition for customers; internal and external objectives don't have to be regarded as mutually exclusive. As well as being concerned with targets such as boosting sales and customer acquisition, marketing activity can also help meet another corporate objective: staff retention. This helps build customer trust and satisfaction, which, as Chapter 6 illustrates, improves corporate profitability.

MARKETING THAT MOTIVATES

In a corporate landscape densely populated by helplines and call centres, it is not only the headline-grabbing retail brands that can benefit from treating staff as their most important customers. One bad experience with a call centre can see a customer walk away from a particular product or service. That could jeopardize a company's reputation and long-term health. As Nick Wreden writes in *ProfitBrand* (2005: 27), the ripple effect from this experience has the potential to wreak havoc:

> While satisfied customers tell four or five others about pleasant experiences, unhappy customers tell 8–13 others. That number rises exponentially if they air their dissatisfactions on the internet. Those they tell are twice as likely to believe 'negative' information as they are positive news. Most worryingly of all: they will continue to discuss their dissatisfaction for up to 23 years.

Over-promising to customers via advertising while not investing in briefing or training staff on how they can fulfil those brand promises is the most common crime in service businesses. Russ Shaw, Director of Capability and Innovation at O2, comments: 'If a service doesn't work, customers leave in droves. Some mobile operators which grew very quickly have had huge servicing issues and network congestions. We've had customers leave us only to come back, saying "We should have stayed with you."'

It's not just the well-known service brands that need to take this on board either – any company that interacts with customers must work hard to prevent a yawning chasm between service expectation and reality.

One company that delivers on what it promises is Powwow, a water-cooler company owned by Nestlé Waters. Stickers on Powwow water coolers promote the idea of water-cooler chat by inviting workers to 'pick up the phone and chat to us'.

The BBC radio DJ Chris Moyles decided to put this promise to the test. No doubt expecting to be fobbed off by an incompetent call centre employee or stuck on hold, Moyles phoned the number when he was live on air. The Powwow employee answered the phone and chatted to Moyles and two other DJs for a few minutes. In an article in *M&M Europe*, Keshen Teo (2002), the Creative Director at brand consultancy Wolff Olins, wrote: 'Powwow was ecstatic. They couldn't have got two minutes [of ad time] on the BBC for love or money. Nor could they have scripted the encounter in a customer relations handbook. The brand-based recruitment criteria and training had worked.'

In other words, what the advertising on the side of the water cooler offered the staff delivered. The seamlessness of this example is particularly striking because the DJ was trying to catch out the company on its promise.

Enlightened organizations are finding that, if employees are treated in the same way as potential customers rather than as anonymous cogs in a corporate wheel, they will be more determined to go the extra mile.

As Chapter 6 discussed, investing in customer loyalty and focusing on retention lead to profits. This is particularly true in the bloody battleground of retail where high street shops are losing customers to internet-based competitors that can offer competitive prices with none of the risks of face-to-face service. A bedrock of customers who can informally act as evangelists for particular products or services results in higher profit margins: they continue to spend money and pass on their recommendations to others. This word-of-mouth factor is invaluable in an environment overloaded by brand choice.

EMPLOYEES ARE CUSTOMERS TOO...

An advertising campaign is not just viewed by an audience; it is also seen by employees. It can have dramatic ramifications about how workers feel about their company.

McDonald's 'I'm lovin' it' moniker, created by the DDB-owned agency Heye & Partner in Germany, was as much about happy staff as Happy Meals. It now extends to its customers as well: McDonald's launched a 'global casting initiative' in spring 2006 that invited both employees and customers to share what they love in life.

In the UK, it also invested in in-store recruitment advertising to shake off the 'McJobs' image that has haunted it since Douglas Coupland's *Generation X* novel in 1991. The ads point out that a career at McDonald's offers opportunities, flexibility and prospects. As well as attracting potential recruits, the ads also serve as a reminder to those working in McDonald's outlets that their employer takes their career prospects and work/life balance seriously.

Employees are customers too. They need to be wooed to feel attracted enough to a company to go and work there in the first place. They subsequently need to feel good about their company because this affects productivity, length of service and morale.

It is particularly critical for retailers and other service-led businesses to grasp this concept. Many retail staff must adhere to a series of particular steps in customer service, such as greeting, enquiring whether customers need particular assistance or asking if they have a loyalty card. We are all too familiar with the scripts that need to be followed at call centres, which rigidly thank us for our call or try to sell us an extra product while we're on the line, or checkout staff on automatic pilot chirruping 'Do you have a store card?'

The challenge facing companies is to invest in innovative ways to communicate with staff across the company so that the internal message is completely in sync with external communications. Without this, all the previous spadework invested in the right message, segmentation and managing your communications portfolio could go to waste.

It's the consumer experience that counts, and a bad one, if shared, may dissuade other potential customers too.

The following case studies are four examples of companies that have improved their business performance by investing in their employees and championing their contribution. In each one, the idea of putting the staff at the centre of the communications comes across loud and clear.

Case study: Schering-Plough – A remarkable recovery

A message from Schering-Plough's Chairman, President and CEO, Fred Hassan, on the drug company's website reads: 'It all begins with the people.'

Hassan goes on to outline the changes that the company underwent after its sales nosedived and it faced serious financial losses and lawsuits. Respectful communication with staff was at the very heart of this turnaround.

In an interview with PricewaterhouseCoopers for its Ninth Annual CEO Survey, published in 2006, Hassan reflects: 'We had to develop a compelling vision so that Schering-Plough people could believe, with good reason, that we could ultimately win our battles. When an organization comes under stress, the focus often becomes very internal, and people lose their spirit in terms of pulling out of the difficulty.'

Today, with 2005 sales of $9.5 billion and 32,000 employees, Schering-Plough has been reformed under Hassan's leadership and commitment to staff.

He joined head office in New Jersey in April 2003 after a difficult 2002 in which the allergy drug Claritin lost patent protection. At the same time, Schering-Plough faced investigations into the safety of its manufacturing processes. What's more, a question mark hung heavy over the company's previous CEO, who had faced accusations of disclosing information to analysts ahead of the public.

In 2005, however, Hassan's 'new Schering-Plough' announced that its third-quarter profits had tripled year on year. How did Hassan steer such an impressive performance in just a few years?

He started by restructuring the hugely decentralized company into three tightly defined business units: pharma, consumer health care and animal health. This helped it to become one global corporation where everyone was aware of his or her role and contribution. This, in turn, made communicating with staff much easier. The new attitude towards the more unified company was summed up by mini-profiles of staff featured in the company's corporate communications.

In an article by Beth Herskovits published in *PR Week US* on 12 December 2005, Jeff Winton, the company's group VP of global communications, commented: 'We have 32,000 publicists right here in the company. A lot of what we send out to our employees is to equip them to be ambassadors, not only for Schering-Plough, but also the [drug] industry.'

A daily newsletter, *Current*, now disseminates company and industry news – an innovation that has been particularly welcomed by Schering-Plough's sales representatives, who are constantly asked about news stories relating to the drug industry. In the *PR Week* article, Winton remarks: 'Our sales force isn't out there keeping up with the media; they're out there selling products. For us to keep up with the fast pace of business we publish *Current* five days a week. Our management feels strongly that we need to be communicating to each of our employees every day.'

Reflecting on how the role of employees has changed over the years, Hassan told PricewaterhouseCooper's Ninth Annual CEO Survey:

> One of the most difficult things for organizations to grapple with is that employees today want to be listened to as if they were customers. They are stakeholders; they are very important. This is very different than 20 or 30 years ago, when employees were, in effect, the instruments of command-and-control management. Today, people have to be treated differently. The newer generations don't accept the command-and-control approach at all. To succeed, a leader must have empathy. This applies to every industry, service and manufacturing. Is this a new complexity? Yes. It is also a new and promising maturity.

Case study: Tesco – Every little helps

A poster adorning the wall of a Tesco staff lavatory reveals that 'A dripping tap can waste 41 litres of water a day. This could cost your store £350 a year.' Apart from being conscious of environmental concerns, this poster also taps into Tesco's mantra, which is 'Every little helps'.

These three words have emerged to become not just decoration for Tesco's latest poster campaign or TV ad, but the retail giant's very philosophy. Getting staff on board to really understand what 'Every little helps' means has been vital to the supermarket's phenomenal success over the last decade, epitomized by the headline towards the end of 2004 that one in eight retail pounds in the UK is spent at Tesco. The friendly, approachable and consumer-oriented Tesco of today couldn't be farther from its former reputation of a 'pile 'em high, sell 'em cheap' image that dogged it throughout the 1980s.

Tesco overtook Sainsbury's to become the UK's market-leading supermarket in 1995. In 1990, a BJM advertising tracking survey across a sample indicated that only 19 per cent of consumers agreed that Tesco had friendly, approachable staff. By 2000, this had more than doubled, to 40 per cent.

Considering that Tesco today is the biggest private sector employer in the UK, with over 250,000 employees, how Tesco treats its staff will have direct repercussions on the millions of shoppers who choose to spend money at the store every day. As Martin Butler (2005) points out: 'A company that treats its staff as disposable, and doesn't truly value them, will find in return that the staff neither respect nor value the company. Such a state of affairs is a particular problem for a retailer because his or her brand is in their hands. Without staff, a retail brand is nothing.'

When Tesco introduced 'Every little helps' in 1993 via its former ad agency Lowe London – a story told by Sharpe and Bamford's Grand Prix-winning 2000 IPA Effectiveness Paper *How Every Little Helps Was a Big Help to Tesco* – it recognized that the secret to its success would be consumers seeing it in action. The philosophy was regarded as a motivating way to train staff and was launched to staff via a video entitled 'How you can help with first class service' and introduced by Lord MacLaurin, who was then Tesco's chairman. In it, he commented: 'The new advertising campaign… says quite a lot about our business. "Every little helps" the housewife in so many ways. It's the hundred and one things that we know we can do to make shopping easier for our customer.'

In Tesco staff canteens, the 'Every little helps' series of ads starring Dotty, the customer from hell, would run on loops and the ads were featured in training videos and bulletins issued to staff. Using instantly recognizable advertising and the familiar character instantly engaged staff with training materials and furnished the retailer with an efficient – and effectively free – training tool.

Claire Beale wrote in *Campaign* on 23 September 2005: 'Dotty, played for a decade by Prunella Scales, was a product of the real experiences of the Tesco staff – a combination of all their most awkward customers. The aim was to show that nothing was too much trouble for the Tesco team, and Dotty tested them to their limits, even returning a fish because of its sullen expression.'

The Dotty campaign gave Tesco staff starring roles as the knights in shining armour, and the workforce responded positively to such a representation: research showed that the campaign helped to demonstrate how far Tesco valued the contribution made by its staff, and this in turn made staff feel more well disposed towards their employer.

Despite Dotty retiring in 2004, her legacy remains. When Sir Terry Leahy, Tesco's CEO, announced the retailer's 2005 results on 25 April 2006, he commented: 'When you come in to work at Tesco, it's a very exciting place. We've got lots of young people coming through. They work very hard. They're very proud of the business. They've got tremendous plans that they want to work on. And we've got a good strategy for them.'

Source: IPA Effectiveness Awards, WARC.

Case study: BUPA – The Personal Health Service

BUPA is a global health and care organization with more than 7 million members and over 40,000 employees in 192 countries. In the UK, its private health insurance scheme is one of the most popular – over half of the UK's companies are BUPA customers. BUPA is also the world's largest provider of international expatriate health insurance, supplying cover to people who are in their home country or living and working abroad. Its 'vision statement' is 'Taking care of lives in our hands'.

BUPA's chief executive and former British Airways marketer Val Gooding told *Campaign* on 14 November 2003: 'It is a practical statement and something we try to live by because it can only mean something if it is adopted by the front line.'

WCRS, BUPA's ad agency, created the Personal Health Service proposition in 2000, a story outlined in Golding and Reid's (2004) IPA Effectiveness Paper. Within the organization, the new proposition – which was designed to complement the National Health Service rather than lock horns with it – made a positive impact. It inspired management, helped to reduce staff turnover and raised morale. This resulted in a positive return on investment: for every £1 spent on advertising, the company saw a return of £3.

BUPA has five business units, which operate independently under separate P&Ls. Using the Personal Health Service allowed these units some consistency and acted as an organizing principle. 'We needed a unifying theme', explains Simon Sheard, BUPA's Head of Marketing.

As a provident association, BUPA ploughs any profits that it makes back into improving the service that it provides in its care homes for the elderly, hospitals and health assessment venues, as well as improving the customer experience at BUPA back-end office functions such as call centres.

The Personal Health Service radically improved BUPA's call handling. A Challenger Team blazed the trail by handling a customer's query individually rather than sticking to a specific script. This paved the way for BUPA to establish a relationship with the customer rather than treating the call as a mere transaction.

Thanks to the improved morale, call centre staff satisfaction rates increased between 1999 and 2002 from 58 per cent to 76 per cent and they have continued to rise since. Sheard says: 'Customer satisfaction rates have steadily improved over the last six years because we have trained our staff to be the kind of people who can answer the question the first time without having to pass callers around the organization.'

He elaborates: 'Our staff are our product. BUPA's front-line staff deliver our promise. It would be easy for me to say that BUPA has the best hospitals and consultants and to list our credentials, but to prove that day in day out on the ground requires our people to live it. It has to be engrained into the organization.'

Extending the 'personal' theme, staff in BUPA care homes are judged against a scheme called 'personal best', while employees are encouraged to broaden their understanding of what BUPA offers its customers by shadowing staff in other disciplines.

Staff turnover has also improved. Over half of BUPA's workforce are caring staff at hospitals and care homes and, in this environment, ensuring that employees are – and remain – motivated, coupled with maintaining a low staff turnover, is particularly important. If this isn't achieved, staffing gaps have to be plugged by temporary agency carers who, in Sheard's opinion, 'aren't as committed and don't live the values'. Agency staff also tend to be a costly alternative. Since the Personal Health Service started weaving its magic within BUPA, agency usage has been eradicated in most care homes.

Across all departments, staff turnover rates decreased from 23 per cent in 1999 to 18 per cent in 2002 across all departments. Since BUPA estimated that it costs £8,000 to replace the average staff member and it now employs around 44,000 staff, recruitment costs in 2002 were £16 million lower than they were in 1999, creating a huge saving for the business.

There is another benefit too. Sheard says:

> We've also found that, as we are a well-run organization, through word of mouth, coupled with advertising that positions BUPA as a leader, interest in joining BUPA is much higher now than a few years ago. We are a Times Top 100 Company to Work For thanks to the way we operate and our commitments to the environment, diversity and work/life balance. This coherent story is helping BUPA to attract many more people.

This is backed up by *The Times*, which reports in the 2006 edition of its Top 100 Companies to Work For report that 84 per cent of BUPA staff applaud the firm's values, believe in the organization's principles and praise its strong team spirit.

Source: IPA Effectiveness Awards, WARC.

Case study: Halifax – The 'X' factor

One trend that has emerged in recent years is to feature employees in advertising campaigns. This tactic has been used by the UK DIY retailer B&Q, as well as Barclays Bank.

The advertiser that is most famous for this strategy in the UK is the Halifax, led by the inimitable contribution made by Howard Brown, a member of staff from the Halifax Sheldon branch, who shot to fame after starring in the bank's ads.

As Richard Warren (2002) notes, in 2000 the Halifax bank wasn't front of mind for consumers opening new bank accounts. So it embarked on a plan of Extraordinary Growth to help jolt it into action. In 2001, it aimed to double the number of current accounts held at the bank by targeting 'switchers' – consumers who held current accounts with other banks – with a hard-to-resist offer. It also planned to tempt consumers with deals on credit cards and mortgages. To stand out from the crowd, Halifax decided to speak like a retailer in its marketing communications, rather than adopt the dry tone adopted by the majority of financial services companies.

Crucially, it recognized that Halifax staff – or 'colleagues' as they are known within the organization – were an important tool in this strategy. Today, around 85 per cent of Halifax sales come from the branch network, and 55 per cent of colleagues are customer-facing. Ensuring that they were motivated via the communications would facilitate business success.

Richard Warren, Group Strategy Director at Delaney Lund Knox Warren and Partners (DLKW) reflects: 'We knew from the outset that it would take more than an advertising idea to transform a 35,000-person organization. We needed a communications idea that had the potential to inform everything Halifax did, both internally and externally.'

A decision was made to use Halifax staff to demonstrate to Halifax's large workforce how important they were. A competition to recruit the bank's born performers was launched on 18 October 2000 by the TV presenter Jonathan Ross on Halifax TV – a weekly broadcast to all staff. Budding stars were then requested to come forward and audition if they were interested. There were 1,169 people who applied and, after eight regional castings, 20 appeared in a national final.

Three colleagues were chosen: Howard Brown from the Sheldon branch, Yvonne McBride from Belfast and Matt Thornfield from the Trinity Road branch in Halifax. In each case, a popular song was chosen and the lyrics were rewritten around a specific Halifax product. Howard extolled the virtues of the high-interest current account to the tune of Tom Jones's 'Sex Bomb'; Yvonne promoted credit cards to the tune of Ricky Martin's 'Livin' La Vida Loca' and Matt sang about mortgages to the tune of the Baha Men's 'Who Let the Dogs Out'.

Results showed that the Howard commercial in particular achieved massive cut-through, but all three ads enjoyed higher recognition than those of the big four banks. By October, the advertising had achieved 86 per cent recognition, and all three ads prompted consumers to shortlist the products. An internal e-mail survey showed that 76 per cent of colleagues agreed with the statement 'The campaign presents colleagues in a positive way'; 85 per cent believed the campaign had given Halifax real momentum, while 78 per cent thought that the campaign had made Halifax a real competitor to other high street banks.

Throughout the year, Howard, Yvonne and Matt starred in the Halifax internal magazine, attended branch openings and appeared on product literature and at staff conferences. New ads were even timed to be launched at key sales conferences throughout the year.

The following year, 1,851 colleagues attended the audition to star in the following year's campaign. Enthusiasm to be the next Howard hasn't waned within Halifax either: this figure shot up to 1,900 at the 2005 auditions, which recruited 12 new stars.

In 2005, DLKW recruited a group of real-life AA patrolmen to star in the breakdown service's TV ad. This time, the staff sang along to 'You've got a friend'. But using employees isn't a sure-fire strategy for a service brand, according to Warren. He dismisses the Barclays campaign that features actors posing as employees, describing them as 'fairly idiotic creatures coming up with completely absurd ideas deemed to be sparks of genius'. He adds: 'Our principle is that we want staff to look good. In any service-based organization, you have the internal morale benefit of using staff, but from the consumer's point of view, if you're using your staff to market the brand, consumers believe that staff are at the heart of the brand. The more motivated employees are, the happier customers are.'

Source: IPA Effectiveness Awards, WARC.

OUR MARKETING ROI STARS AND THEIR EMPLOYEES

Our Marketing ROI stars offer further inspiration of how to build profitability through investing in marketing that motivates staff as well as customers.

When O2 launched, it was as much about spreading the gospel to its workforce as it was to drum up new business. As Susie Moore, O2's UK Head of Brand and Marketing Communications, comments: 'The launch of O2 was about the company as a proposition; internally it gave people a new lease of life. Our whole philosophy was that the brand wasn't about the advertising; it was about a philosophy and an approach. Employees are so key to building the brand; it has to start from them.'

Even in a sprawling multinational organization like P&G – which has nearly 98,000 employees working in 80 countries worldwide – a successful brand vision can still work to unite people and give them the momentum they need to work towards the same objectives. In P&G's case, it refers to this as 'people power'. Even as far back as 1947, Richard Deupree, a former P&G CEO, famously said: 'If you leave us our money, our buildings and our brands, but take away our people, the company will fail. But if you take away our money, our buildings and our brands, but leave us our people, we can rebuild the whole thing in a decade.'

One other way in which employees are increasingly motivated is through corporate social responsibility (CSR). Staff turnover at Microsoft in the UK, for instance, is just 11 per cent, and this, many believe, is linked to the corporation's philanthropic nature, which is led from the top. Bill Gates, the founder, even announced his decision to go part time in June 2006. Gates plans to devote himself to the Bill and Melinda Gates Foundation, which invests billions in world health problems. The philanthropic culture is well understood throughout Microsoft: in *The Times* 100 Best Companies to Work For report in 2006, 84 per cent of staff at Microsoft UK believed that the organization made a positive difference to the world.

CSR activity can certainly motivate staff and make them feel good about where they work, but there is no substitute for well-managed communication throughout the organization. Employees need to understand common goals and their role in helping to achieve them. Creating a common vision and seeing how their contribution fits in empowers staff.

Smart marketing investment portfolio managers work hard to assist that process of empowerment. If managed correctly, it will deliver contented staff, loyal customers and a compound return. As Scott Bedbury, the former Marketing Officer of Starbucks, points out (2002: 133): 'The challenge for any company is not to simply create a nice place to work, but to create an environment that embodies the core values of the brand, both explicitly and implicitly. There is no place more important to communicate brand values than in front of every employee every day.'

13

Is your organization Marketing ROI-fit?

How marketing organizations and marketing service agencies can realize a Marketing ROI agenda

When asked what he would like from his marketing staff to enable them to be more mission-critical to his company's performance, Ian Edwards, the Finance Director at UK retailer Comet, didn't skip a beat. He replied: 'If we could bridge that understanding in terms of ROI for the different media types or activities that would be the single biggest factor. That would give us greater confidence that more expenditure can deliver higher returns.'

In this chapter, we show the confidence that being ROI-fit can afford – not just to marketers and their boards, but also their agency partners.

Remember the eight investor tips to profitable marketing communications:

1. Concentrate on outcomes, not outputs.
2. Forget consumers, target customers.
3. Manage your communication investment portfolio.

4. Differentiate any way you can.
5. Engagement and experience are the new 30-second ads.
6. Apply a 'focus investing' approach.
7. Establish a measurement culture.
8. Leverage your employee capital.

Any company that is able to follow these tips with help from the previous chapters in this book is already making great strides in becoming ROI-fit. As we have already covered those tips in some detail, we devote this chapter to other issues, such as internal structural and cultural challenges, as well as effective agency management.

WHY ROI IS IMPORTANT

Most major advertisers spend as much on promoting their brands as they earn from them. Procter & Gamble, for instance, spends between 10 and 12 per cent of its sales on advertising. It makes about the same amount every year in profits. For instance, in 2005, it made profits of $7,257 million on revenues of $56,741 million. Its marketing budget for the same year was approximately $6,000 million.

TNS Media figures for 2005 show that P&G, the biggest US advertiser, spent over a tenth of its profits in the United States alone: $793.8 million. Meanwhile, the second-biggest US advertiser, General Motors, spent $706 million. While average ad spending increased by 5.2 per cent in 2005, the top 10 ad spenders boosted their ad revenue by 6.9 per cent.

With hundreds of millions of dollars being spent by individual companies, CEOs are perfectly within their rights to question whether the spend is worth it, even when there is strong evidence to suggest that a particular marketing strategy is working. Marketing ROI is being challenged in boardrooms across the globe, not just because of the scale of the amounts involved, but also because companies understandably want to make good decisions in terms of driving future growth.

Our experience is that marketing professionals are motivated to drive a Marketing ROI agenda, but in doing so find themselves confronting huge hurdles, not least within their own organizations. Corporate structures, cultures or modi operandi sometimes just don't allow the freedom or discipline for an organization to become ROI-fit.

Below, we outline five ways to help any organization become more focused on ROI.

1. CEOs and CMOs: sharing the agenda

Considering that it's up to CEOs to grow an organization, marketing shouldn't be something that they delegate; they should be actively involved in setting the agenda. This is not just for the marketing team's benefit; a CEO who is plugged into how the company can create demand for its products and services is incredibly influential when it comes to encouraging investors to buy stock.

It's perhaps no coincidence that Sir Terry Leahy, the CEO of Tesco, comes from a marketing background; the retail group's resurgence in the 1990s and 2000s was in part driven by successful marketing, spearheaded by initiatives such as Clubcard, described in Chapter 6.

CEOs who are close to the marketing process also tend to be close to their front line and have Leahy's understanding of how to focus a company on customers. When management has a clear vision of what marketing is expected to deliver, it's not just marketing that benefits; the entire organization can profit.

In our experience, Marketing ROI is less likely to work if the CMO is given carte blanche just to 'get on with it'. In this scenario, the strategy or execution is challenged too late, or marketing suffers from not getting sufficient support. Strong leadership and direction are required.

Only CEOs can make trade-offs in the business because only they can truly know the intricate details of the bigger picture in terms of whether company resources are best invested in marketing as opposed to, say, training or IT. The CEO doesn't need to come from a marketing background, as in Leahy's case, but *does* need to be clear about what he or she wants marketing to achieve.

A CMO who is commercially minded and has a strong alignment with the CEO and the board is critical. And a CMO who has credibility on the board is essential if the CEO isn't a hands-on marketer.

A survey of 370 listed companies in the United States by the Association of National Advertisers and the consultancy Booz Allen Hamilton in 2004 found that the CMO's role is poorly defined at many companies. What's more, the CMO position is present in just 47 per cent of Fortune 100 companies as opposed to chief financial officer (91 per cent), chief human resources officer (83 per cent) and chief information officer (80 per cent).

It's not essential for marketers to have a presence on the board as long as there is a marketing-savvy CEO who can assist marketing to focus on outcomes related to the business. And an organization that is Marketing ROI-fit *is* focused on outcomes, not on second-guessing management.

Too many marketers can find themselves spending far too much time trying to work the system in their organization rather than focusing on how best to achieve results.

What every marketer wants from the CEO...

- *CEOs who are brand champions.* When CEOs are particularly visible, like Bill Gates or Richard Branson, they market the company through hitting the headlines and being opinionated, open and passionate. The ideal scenario is when marketing becomes a corporate mission rather than just a series of product claims. As discussed in Chapter 12, when a genuine mission is positively incorporated into a company it makes a positive contribution. Think of Tesco's 'Every little helps' or BUPA's Personal Health Service. Each mission penetrated the company, serving as a rallying cry. Once there is buy-in from staff, profits follow.
- *CEOs need to support the CMOs in making big bets on high-probability events.* A commitment to narrowing the scale of investments needs to be supported from the top. Strong leadership is required to give the final word on accountability and to help define metrics. If CEOs don't offer their input, it is hardly surprising that marketing does not achieve its desired outcomes.

2. Breaking down silos

In Chapter 11, we showed how Samsung confronted the control that country managers had on their marketing budgets head on to achieve an impressive ROI.

ROI-fit marketing departments need to break away from defending their territory and instead operate as cross-functional as opposed to specialist departments. They need to get buy-in from stakeholders – the first stage in the 'how to focus on outcome-led marketing' process outlined in Chapter 5.

Being cross-functional means that marketing, sales and customer service teams share information and expertise rather than operating in splendid isolation. It also entails implementing common metrics that have meaning across several departments. If finance, sales, operations and personnel can see the value of marketing first-hand via easily understood and transferable metrics, organizations will become more streamlined.

Everyone in an organization has a stake in the brand and what it can achieve in terms of driving value. So it follows that every single stakeholder needs to be able to see the progress that the brand is making. Separate campaigns organized by different departments create a lack of clarity in a brand's communication, and that can hamper Marketing ROI. Gillette, for instance, which owned Oral B and Duracell, did not create a battery-powered toothbrush until people working on the two brands broke down internal silos and started talking to each other.

Financial services institutions are often guilty of working in silos. One particularly potent example comes from a US bank whose marketing goal was to increase customer loyalty by offering them the convenience of having all their accounts in one place. The reality was a different matter altogether.

Those customers who did have multiple accounts received statements for each one rather than a consolidated statement, and in-branch staff couldn't tell how many different accounts a customer had. The bank was divided into individual profit centres that all clashed with each other, so customers were often not told about a particular savings plan that generated from a different department, even when it may have been a much more appropriate option for them.

The different departments were all rewarded on sales rather than on customer satisfaction or retention, meaning that customers lost out at the expense of staff hitting the numbers – output-based marketing on a chronic scale.

3. Continuity of marketing departments

Whether the high turnover of CMOs is adding to the declining influence of marketing or is merely symptomatic of it is neither here nor there. The point is that having CMOs *in situ* for an average length of 22.9 months is disruptive to establishing an ROI culture where the focus incorporates the long-term payback of marketing campaigns.

So why do marketers leave after two or three years?

Part of it comes down to unrealistic expectations of what marketing will deliver. When a new CMO joins, past experience, learnings and insight are often sidelined in favour of a new marketing agenda and possibly a pitch process to recruit new agency partners. A new CMO may change the metrics, resulting in a lack of continuity. Here is where a hands-on CEO may prove invaluable in protecting the contribution of a predecessor.

The value of CMOs spending longer in a marketing role is being realized by marketing-savvy organizations. P&G, for instance, which pioneered the two-year brand manager role, has now moved towards longer assignments by brand managers, lasting up to four years. This means that a consistency will be built up over time, and the benefits will be clear to future brand managers on those products, so they may not be so quick to dispense with them on arrival.

The consistency of how P&G plans, measures, manages and evaluates its brands allows for a smoother transition when brand managers move on.

The dangers of being inconsistent are many and varied. The example given in Chapter 10 of Smirnoff vodka and how its 14 separate campaigns helped to open the market up to rival marques conveniently contrasts with Absolut. The Swedish vodka brand built up its presence in the United States through a consistent print campaign.

4. Create a Marketing ROI culture

For companies that are serious about becoming Marketing ROI-fit, the following six points, which we have referred to over the course of the book, offer guidance in terms of measuring the right things, as well as ensuring there is company-wide support and buy-in:

- a portfolio approach to marketing investment that empowers decision making and budget allocation assessment;
- a culture of accountability that is welcomed rather than resisted by marketers;
- senior management helping to decide on metrics that link up with company strategy and which can be used across the organization;
- easy access to intelligence about where to shift funds for optimum effectiveness;
- an open attitude towards experimentation;
- a commitment to long-term metrics such as lifetime value as opposed to an over-reliance on short-term metrics such as sales data.

Some organizations are even introducing specific roles to ensure that ROI is top of the marketing agenda. At Lloyds TSB, Julian Elliott's official title is Head of Group Marketing Effectiveness, and his task is to input into all marketing areas across departments to fast-track improvements in ROI. He explains: 'My role is to work as part of a cross-functional team and as part of both the finance and the marketing departments.'

We support this kind of role within organizations because it can only serve to improve ROI fitness levels.

Another improvement is in building and managing databases to help focus on retaining rather than acquiring customers. Without such data providing insight into customer behaviour and transactions, personalized communication remains a pipe dream rather than an achievable reality.

5. Managing your agencies more effectively

You get out of an agency what you put in. When I go into a meeting room and see poor creative work, there's no point getting deflated. I know what they can do. I've seen the quality stuff before. Perhaps it was the brief that was at fault. You both need to work hard at what you want from the relationship.

Colin Green, Global Marketing Director,
Land Rover, in *Campaign*, 27 May 2005

Why is it that an ad agency can produce show-stopping and engaging ads that move the needle for one client, yet the same agency working on a different client can produce a piece of communication that commits the deadliest sin of all: not being remembered? Perhaps there's more than a nugget of truth in the saying that clients get the advertising that they deserve.

Case study: P&G – A true agency partnership

The best marketing communications come from a partnership between clients and agencies. As Bernhard Glock, the Global Media and Communications Manager for Procter & Gamble, points out in Chapter 7, collaboration is what drives success.

P&G enjoys a healthy relationship with its ad agencies because both parties understand that the strategic business objective hinges on growth. P&G pays its agencies on the basis of the sales uplift of their brands, a commission structure that is linked to performance not to spend, in other words to outcome as opposed to output. P&G is always happy to pay its agencies more money – but only if they work for it and can demonstrate that their contributions have grown the business.

P&G pays its agencies on a percentage of sales rather than on a percentage of media spending or on resource. This offers agencies a clear incentive to think about purely media advertising spending rather than marketing through multiple channels. P&G also pays its agencies globally, encouraging them to think globally, as well as empowering them to question and challenge their thinking. P&G doesn't have a culture of months and months spent pitching. Instead, it will award work on an agency's track record with existing assignments. Toyota works in a similar fashion, demonstrating its commitment to its agency partners.

All of our Marketing ROI stars demonstrate a pattern of allowing their agencies to interpret the brief, challenge it and return to them with their thoughts. This indicates a respect for the agencies' wealth of experience in different sectors that could feed into a differentiating strategy. Agencies are also trained to take the consumer perspective and don't have company politics and corporate culture obstructing their vision.

LEARNING FROM THE PITCH

Many marketers often feel that they only get fresh ideas from their agency if they put their business up for pitch. They believe that the competitive environment gets the best people on the account and improves the focus of their agency. By the same token, agencies believe they receive better briefings, access to the different executives even beyond marketing decision makers and a much more focused client.

The pitching process often allows for agencies to challenge the brief, but this tends to happen much less frequently in day-to-day account management. Pitches emphasize quality of briefing and an open attitude towards new ideas, but this needs to become engrained into a client–agency relationship if it is to enjoy longevity and work that delivers on ROI objectives.

RELATIONSHIP MANAGEMENT

A common description of most client–agency relationships is that agencies have lost their place at the top table; in other words, responsibility for advertising has been delegated down the pecking order in so many organizations that there's often a rigidity in the relationship. Agencies don't see clients who approve the work as often as they used to. Meanwhile, marketers would benefit from more regular contact with the most senior people who work on their account to give them ample opportunity to communicate information about their brands and their business strategies.

Think about the kind of relationship you'd like to have with your marketing services agencies. It's true that ad agencies, PR firms, media specialists, direct marketing companies, digital shops and research consultancies are people-driven organizations, but in the end they are still commercial businesses required to return a profit. If they don't make money, they will eventually reduce their resources – an action that normally entails taking away human resource from a certain account so that they can work on a more 'profitable' one.

Advertising is a competitive business by nature, so when agencies are left to their own devices they find it hard to collaborate. It is in their culture to own their client relationship, the budget, or the lead on strategy.

THE BRIEF

Being tightly briefed gets the process off to a good start. Jeff Goodby, the Co-chairman of Goodby, Silverstein & Partners, uses a fishing analogy to describe the briefing process. Goodby says that a brief should guide people to the right part of the river. It should advise them on the most appropriate type of fly and common behaviours of fish but, crucially, not actually set out to catch the fish. Gladman and Melsom interpret this as providing 'direction but not directives' in their 2005 *Market Leader* article entitled 'Breakthrough creativity: a blend of art and science'.

Focusing on an insight allows all agencies working on communication to translate the insight into a relevant consumer benefit.

UNIFICATION, NOT INTEGRATION

Agencies should be working to unify their agendas as opposed to jostling over which agency should take the lead either by appointment or by assertion. This means that the client ends up with an advertising or direct marketing campaign rather than an idea that can work well across multiple touchpoints.

A strategy that looks past traditional practices and new models to plan Marketing ROI is the best course of action here because it accepts that communication strategy can come from a number of communication partners. Certain clients have fallen into the practice of appointing the ad agency as the default lead agency, but there are several options open to the client. Creative, media, direct marketing, integrated, PR, field marketing, digital and modelling specialists could all support, input to or lead the communications strategy.

HOW DOES THE AD INDUSTRY
NEED TO CHANGE?

In Chapter 1, we stressed the need for a new marketing model. In subsequent chapters, we have considered what steps marketers can take to address their needs. But ad agencies are not immune to the need for change either, particularly if they are to become more ROI-smart for the benefit of their clients.

Currently, ROI is not in most agencies' DNA. Part of this is down to an awards culture that celebrates creativity at the expense of effectiveness. Lloyds TSB's Julian Elliott is flabbergasted at the number of awards schemes: 'Advertising has more awards ceremonies than I've seen in any other industry, possibly more than all the other industries on the planet put together.'

A more business-driven approach to communications is required by agencies. ROI needs to become as common in agencies' everyday lexicon as creativity, branding and awareness. Otherwise they risk not adding value and clients will cut back on the contribution that their agencies currently make in favour of more accountable ones.

SELLING ADVERTISING

Just as marketers need to be able to sell the idea of marketing to their boards, advertising agencies need to be able to sell the case for advertising. Many agencies will boast that they are 'media-neutral' in their credentials, but how many do you hear describing themselves as 'investment-neutral'? Yet companies need a business – rather than a creative – case for investing in advertising. A communications strategy needs to lead to creative solutions, and should make just as much sense to the CFO as the CMO.

Agencies also need to understand that branding is not the only answer. Indeed branding competes with other expenditures that could generate a much more impressive return on investment than brand-led activity.

There is still a time and a place for image-building and brand-awareness advertising, but they are no longer dominant. Agencies that once focused on 30-second commercials are now branching out into events, websites, direct marketing, sales promotion and sponsorship, as well as monitoring emerging channels. Metrics such as awareness are very much a legacy from the branding movement that is now being eclipsed by other marketing strategies. The industry needs a new set of advertising metrics to reflect the shift from traditional media to non-media channels, as well as the move away from customer acquisition focus to building customer satisfaction and loyalty.

BUILDING VALUE

All CEOs want to build shareholder value, and companies are valued not on their current earnings but on their potential for growth. During a recession, many companies automatically cut costs, but the more savvy ones improve top-line organic growth by stimulating demand, increasing market share, launching new products and entering new markets. For instance, Morgan Stanley started an extensive globalization programme in 1993 and, despite criticism from analysts, stuck to its guns and continued to invest in troubled economies such as Mexico and Russia, both of which were going through debt crises. Yet in the mid-1990s, the firm took large amounts of market share and added 15 per cent to its headcount – proof that hunkering down and slashing costs during difficult times is not the only option available to companies, despite it being an understandable and natural reflex.

The advertising industry can help its clients by having a firm view on its role and its value in their business objectives at a strategic level. Ad agencies can show not only marketing directors, but also finance directors and CEOs, the contribution they can make in helping to build shareholder value.

EQUIPPING AGENCIES TO DELIVER A MARKETING ROI AGENDA

Compare advertising with almost any other industry – information technology, retail or travel, to name but three – and it's easy to see how it has remained largely the same, despite some revolutionary changes taking place among its client companies.

These changes include restructuring, outsourcing or offshoring, and technological advance. In some cases, technology has even prompted a new business model. Consider how travel agents are rapidly becoming an anachronism. A Mintel report, *Travel Agents – UK*, published in December 2004, showed that just 31 per cent of overseas trips were booked in person.

A NEW BREED OF AGENCIES

Advertising has to reconfigure its role, and that's no mean feat. Andrew Singer, the Finance and Systems Director at Toyota GB, comments: 'Advertising is so wrapped up in its own history that it seems not to want to move along with the rest of industry.'

One major stumbling block is the fact that advertising sees itself as a creative industry, but to stay in business it has to answer to a higher order, which is business accountability. New agency models are starting to cater to the needs of industry, for instance Anomaly, a New York-based hotshop that works with the likes of Coca-Cola and Virgin America.

In praise of Anomaly, Spence Kramer, the VP, Marketing and Communications at Virgin America, commented to *Campaign* on 5 May 2006: 'With a traditional agency, nine times out of ten, the solution is an ad. At Anomaly, they're product-focused; it's not always about communications. They dig into every aspect of our business, from arm-rests to uniforms.' And the agency insists on being paid on the strength of its ideas as opposed to time sheets, preferring to be paid in terms of royalties or share of revenue. Surely such a business model is more conducive to pushing ROI higher up the agency agenda.

Challenges for agencies wanting to become more ROI-fit include shifting the emphasis from counting media impressions to making connections with consumers. This can be achieved by agencies placing more onus on interactive communication and one-to-one relationships through experience-enhancing media like the internet and mobile devices. A real strength of agencies is their ability to come up with ideas that enhance experiences and that differentiate one brand from another. But their weakness is backing up these strategies with measurement. If they want to become more ROI-fit, they need to investigate more holistic solutions that extend beyond traditional media and alter how they measure these touchpoints.

Agencies also need to recognize that existing, not new, customers are where much of the profit is for their clients. They need to be able to beef up their insight into and experience of existing customers and to mine data into that customer base to help identify possible competitive advantages. The technology to drive that and the customers already exist; agencies' future revenue streams could heavily rely on bridging the gap.

The example of Anomaly stands out because its business model is geared towards earning as much revenue from strategy as from implementation. Yet it is the exception to the rule. Agencies usually give away their strategy for nothing and will invoice their clients for implementation costs. Until they are able to earn remuneration for their strategy, it will be difficult for them to wrestle their current position of an agency–client vendor relationship back to that of an agency–client partnership.

This remains a particular challenge considering that the current business model and structure tend to favour the creation of traditional advertising and media solutions over strategic ones.

If all ad agencies were able to offer more sophisticated data analytics that were capable of anticipating what the consumer is likely to want most and do next – as many direct and digital agencies already do – they would become much more ROI-fit in the eyes of marketers and CEOs, and consequently be taken more seriously as businesses.

And if they invested more in post-campaign analysis that incorporated real-time feedback from consumer panels rather than pretesting, they would help their clients to reduce the risk of a campaign. This would help clients to evaluate and optimize their campaigns and would discipline agencies to be more analytical and skilled in terms of how they use data. This already happens in other creative industries such as film and TV, where the creative aspect is outsourced and film and TV businesses evaluate and manage a fiscal result.

Finally, if agencies worked collaboratively, they would find that they could in fact share data, expertise and insights on common clients. There has been talk around integration for many years now but, if agencies are going to become serious about Marketing ROI, a preferable strategy is one that endorses a *unified* approach. Marketers who want to improve their ROI fitness are seeking collaborative specialists who are unified by common strategy, metrics and vision for their brand. If agencies – from whatever discipline – are able to adapt their offering to match that need, they will be protecting their future income.

SUMMARY

Marketing ROI is not just an alternative term for 'effectiveness', 'impact' or 'results'. Nor is it a magic equation or formula.

It is an attitude about creating profit.

Marketing ROI is about driving growth. This can be done through short-term improvements in cash flow or via capital gains thanks to winning customers' trust and confidence. Both of these outcomes will evolve into long-term profit.

Finally, Marketing ROI is about the smart investment of marketing funds.

Happy investing.

References

Aaker, DA (1996) *Building Strong Brands*, Free Press, New York

Accenture (2004) *High Performance Workforce Study, 2002–2003*, Accenture, Palo Alto, CA

Ambler, T (2004) *Marketing and the Bottom Line*, 2nd edn, FT Prentice Hall, Harlow

Association of National Advertisers (ANA)/Blueprint Communications (2006) *Integrated Marketing Communications Survey Results*, ANA, New York

Association of National Advertisers (ANA)/Booz Allen Hamilton (2004) *Are CMOs Irrelevant? Organization, accountability and the new marketing agenda*, Booz Allen Hamilton, New York

Barwise, P and Styler, A (2003) *The Marketing Expenditure Trends Report*, London Business School, London

Bedbury, S (2002) *A New Brand World*, Penguin Putnam, New York

Blattberg, R and Deighton, J (1996) Manage marketing by the customer equity test, *Harvard Business Review*, July

Butler, M with Gravatt, S (2005) *People Don't Buy What You Sell, They Buy What You Stand For*, Management Books 2000, Cirencester

Clancy, K and Stone, R (2005) Don't blame the metrics, *Harvard Business Review*, June

Corstjens, M and Merrihue, J (2003) Optimal marketing, *Harvard Business Review*, October

Court, C, Gordon, J and Perrey, J (2005) Boosting returns on marketing investment, *McKinsey Quarterly*, 2

Day, R, Storey, R and Edwards, A (2004) *BA: Climbing above the turbulence – how British Airways countered the budget airline threat*, Institute of Practitioners in Advertising (IPA) Effectiveness Paper, IPA, London

Ephron, E and Pollak, G (2003) Finding the other half, Paper presented at the ARF/ESOMAR Conference, June

Forrester Research and the Association of National Advertisers (ANA) (2004) *Defining ROI*, Forrester Research, Cambridge, MA

Gladman, P and Melsom, A (2005) Breakthrough creativity: a blend of art and science, *Market Leader*, 31, Winter

Golding, D and Reid, J (2004) *Bupa Personal Health Service*, IPA Effectiveness Paper, IPA, London

Heath, R and Nairn, A (2005) Measuring effective advertising: implications of low attention processing on recall, *Journal of Advertising Research*, **45** (2), June

Hopkins, C (1980 [1923]) *Scientific Advertising*, Chelsea House, New York

Jones, JP (1995) *When Ads Work: New proof that advertising triggers sales*, Simon & Schuster/Lexington Books

Kotler, P (2002) *Marketing Management: Analysis, planning, implementation and control*, Prentice Hall, Upper Saddle River, NJ

KPMG International (2006) *Rethinking the Business Model*, Economist Intelligence Unit, London

Kumar, N (2004) *Marketing as Strategy: Understanding the CEO's agenda for driving growth and innovation*, Harvard Business School Press, Boston, MA

Lance, A (2006) My most contagious idea, *Contagious*, 7

LaPointe, P (2003) Marketing ROI: where are you on the ladder of insight?, *MarketingNPV*, **1** (2)

Leahy, T (2005) A picture of people power, in D Franklin (ed), *The World in 2006*, Economist, London

Lowenstein, M (2003) Examining the emerging reality of the impact of employee loyalty on customer service, *Customer Relationship Management*, 8 (3)

McGovern, G et al (2004) Bringing customers into the boardroom, *Harvard Business Review*, November

Maunder, S et al (2004) *O2: It only works if it all works – how troubled BT Cellnet transformed into thriving O2*, IPA Effectiveness Paper, IPA, London

Miller, A and Cioffi, J (2004) Measuring marketing effectiveness and value: the Unisys marketing dashboard, *Journal of Advertising Research*, 44 (3)

Mintel (2004) *Travel Agents – UK*, Mintel, London

Mintel (2006a) *Coffee – UK*, Mintel, London

Mintel (2006b) *Health and Fitness Clubs – US*, Mintel, Chicago

Moore, B and Allsop, D (2004) The ROI imperative: how to build measurable value, Paper presented at the ESOMAR Annual Congress, September, Lisbon

Nail, J (2005) Where is marketing measurement headed: a survey of the members of the Association of National Advertisers Survey, *Forrester*, 13 January

Nicholls, W and Raillard, G (2004) *Lynx Pulse: Proving the value of integration*, IPA Effectiveness Paper, IPA, London

Olins, W (2006) Branding nations, *Contagious*, 6

Porter, M (2001) Now is the time to rediscover strategy, *Does Strategy Really Matter Anymore?*, *EBF*, 8, Winter, European Business Forum

Reichheld, F (2001 [1996]) *The Loyalty Effect: The hidden force behind growth, profits, and lasting value*, rev edn, Harvard Business School Press, Boston, MA

Reichheld, F (2003) The one number you need to grow, *Harvard Business Review*, December

Roberts, K (2004) *Lovemarks: The future beyond brands*, Powerhouse Books, New York

Robertson, P (1998) New brand development, in *Brands: The new wealth creators*, ed S Hart and J Murphy, pp 24–32, Macmillan Press, London

Schwartz, B (2005) *The Paradox of Choice: Why more is less: how the culture of abundance robs us of satisfaction*, Harper Perennial, New York

Scott, F (2006) Integrated viewpoints, *Marketing Week*, April

Sharpe, A and Bamford, J (2000) *How Every Little Helps Was a Big Help to Tesco*, IPA Effectiveness Paper, IPA, London

Sherrington, M (2003) *Added Value: The alchemy of brand-led growth*, Palgrave Macmillan, Basingstoke, New York

Storey, R (2005) Defying commoditisation in your market, in *Advertising Works and How: Winning communication strategies for business*, ed L Green, World Advertising Research Centre, Oxfordshire

Teo, K (2002) What's truth got to do with it?, *M&M Europe*, December

Trout, J (2000) *Differentiate or Die: Survival in our era of killer competition*, John Wiley, New York

VanBoskirk, S (2005) *Left Brain Marketing Planning*, 16 May, Forrester Research, Cambridge, MA

Warren, R (2002) *HBOS: Taking on the high street banks by communicating like a high street retailer*, IPA Effectiveness Paper, IPA, London

Wreden, N (2005) *ProfitBrand: How to increase the profitability, accountability and sustainability of brands*, Kogan Page, London

Further reading

Baker, S and Mitchell, H (2002) *Integrated Marketing Communications*, ESOMAR, Amsterdam

Binet, L (2005) Evaluating marketing communications: a guide to best practice, *Market Leader*, Summer

Blair, M and Kuse, A (2004) Better practices in advertising can change a cost of doing business to wise investments in the business, *Journal of Advertising Research*, 44, March

Briggs, R (2006) Quantifying Marketing ROI: the Philips journey, *Admap*, 469, February

Collins, J (2001) *Good to Great: Why some companies make the leap... and others don't*, Random House Business Books, London

Kapferer, J-N (2004) *The New Strategic Brand Management: Creating and sustaining brand equity long term*, Kogan Page, London

Lewis, D and Bridger, D (2001) *The Soul of the New Consumer: Authenticity: what we buy and why in the new economy*, Nicholas Brealey Publishing, London

Mendelsohn, T (2006) Trends 2006, *Multichannel Retail*, Forrester, Cambridge, MA

Nail, J (2005) *Best Practices in Market Mix Modeling*, 25 August, Forrester Research, Cambridge, MA

O'Halloran, P and Mosher, P (2003) *Marketing: Underrated, undervalued, and unimportant*, 10 September, Accenture, Palo Alto, CA

Shaw, R (2005) How to demonstrate marketing's profitability, *Market Leader*, Summer

Shelton, D and O'Gorman, R (2003) *Advertisers Disappointed with Marketing Integration*, Blueprint Communications, in collaboration with the Association of National Advertisers, March

Tier, M (2004) *The Winning Investment Habits of Warren Buffett and George Soros*, Inverse Books, Hong Kong

Index